From Civility to Survival: Richmond Ladies During the Civil War

From Civility to Survival: Richmond Ladies During the Civil War

The Ladies reveal their wartime private thoughts and struggles in compelling diaries and emotional memories.

NEAL E. WIXSON

iUniverse, Inc.
Bloomington

From Civility to Survival: Richmond Ladies During the Civil War
The Ladies reveal their wartime private thoughts and struggles in compelling diaries and emotional memories.

The print on the cover "Richmond Ladies going to receive Government Rations—Don't you think that Yankee must feel like shrinking in his boots before such high-toned Southern Ladies as we?" by A.R. Waud is courtesy of the Library of Congress.

iUniverse books may be ordered through booksellers or by contacting:

iUniverse
1663 Liberty Drive
Bloomington, IN 47403
www.iuniverse.com
1-800-Authors (1-800-288-4677)

ISBN: 978-1-4620-6716-9 (sc)
ISBN: 978-1-4620-6717-6 (ebk)

Printed in the United States of America

iUniverse rev. date: 01/12/2012

CONTENTS

INTRODUCTION

Some historians feel that the role of women in the civil war has been vastly underrated. They clothed the soldiers, entertained the soldiers, cared for the soldiers and facilitated the end of the war by encouraging soldiers to desert their regiments since the cause was lost. In addition, they struggled to survive when their life in all aspects was turned upside down. In many cases, they were forced to abandon their homes as enemy troops approached, only to flee with a limited number of household goods and a small amount of clothing and personal items.

As they abandoned their homes, the refugees, as they were called, had no place to go and no idea as to how long they would be gone. They generally headed to their relative's homes, thinking that their displacement would only be of short duration. After becoming a burden to their relatives, they would move to cities to take advantage of their safety, more housing options, possible jobs and social activities offered. However, as resources became scare in terms of food, shelter, and jobs, the refugees became an increasing burden for the cities and sympathy for them by the citizens lessened.

In their past life, they may have been landowners of some wealth with slaves performing the cooking, cleaning, shopping and other necessary chores. Now, as refugees, they were renters focused on finding the basic necessities of life for themselves. They sacrificed their privacy in rooms renting for high sums of money. They were constantly on the move. Their faith, endurance and courage were tested to the highest degree. Those with children could not assure proper schooling for them. With their loved ones, husbands, sons, and brothers off to war, they became the decision-makers, a role that was new to them. In short, theirs was a life of constant stress, hardship and sacrifice.

What is most impressive is that, despite these circumstances, their focus was to support the war effort by volunteering in so many ways. Even after the war, the Ladies of Richmond focused their efforts on honoring the fallen soldiers and were instrumental in organizing Memorial Day to honor them. They were also instrumental in finding the bodies of their fallen soldiers and returning them to Virginia.

Many did not revert to their former status at the end of the war. They awaited the return of their loved ones. They went to find their plantations and farms ransacked with their crops trampled, and their valuables stolen. Needless to say, there was little money for seed since the confederate money was worthless.

During the war, several women in Richmond kept diaries or notes of their experiences. Their entries or memories provide us a valuable window into their lives. Initially, serving as a record of events, the diaries or notes increasingly served a therapeutic purpose by allowing women to record their feelings and emotions. The primary diarist in this book is Judith McGuire. She kept her diary for over three years in Richmond. Others who speak to us by their writings are Myrta Lockett Avary, Fanny Taylor Dickinson, Constance Cary Harrison, Mary Tucker Magill, Phoebe Yates Pember, and Sallie Brock Putnam. I have selected excerpts with minor edits from their diaries and writings and have not reproduced them in their entirety. My focus in such selecting and editing was their thoughts, emotions and reactions to the changes that they were courageously enduring. They are not the traditional mistresses of the plantation during the civil war. Others have told their stories. These writers are from all strata of society who are ultimately reduced to one. I have included other references for contextual purposes.

I am grateful for receiving assistance and guidance in developing this book. As the extensive research suggests, extraordinary assistance was required to acquire these books. Rebecca Mazzarella of the Staff in the Wolf Law Library at William & Mary Law School was of great help in securing numerous books from the William & Mary Swem Library and others.

Donna Wixson, my wife, the consummate reviewer of manuscripts, provided me with her thoughts and guidance. In addition, John M. Coski, Historian and Director of Library and Research at the Museum of the Confederacy, and Frances Pollard, Chief Librarian of the Virginia Historical Society, were generous with their time and expertise in guiding me through their vast stores of archives. The picture of Judith McGuire is part of the archives of the Virginia Historical Society and was kindly made available to me. The Richmond pictures are courtesy of the United States National Archives and the United States Library of Congress. I must also note the extraordinary assistance given to me by Michael Chesson, Jeff Toalson, Will Molineux, and Carol Sheriff, all gifted civil war writers and lecturers in their own right. Their interest and support have guided me through the journey involved in this process.

PICTURES

Judith White Brockenbrough McGuire, Leading Lady

Constance Cary Harrison, Date and photographer unknown

Mary Tucker Magill, Date and photographer unknown

Phoebe Pember, Date and photographer unknown

View of Richmond, Virginia, 1865, Matthew Brady, photographer

Two Women in Black, April, 1865, Alexander Gardner, photographer

Residence of Jefferson Davis (1201 East Clay Street), April-June, 1865, Photographer unknown

St. Paul's Episcopal Church (Grace Street), April, 1865, John Reekie, photographer

Houses on Governor Street—April 1865, Photographer unknown

St. John's Church and Graveyard from the street, April-June 1865, Photographer unknown

Ruined Buildings in the Burned District, April-June 1865, Photographer unknown

General Edward O.C. Ord, wife and child at the Residence of Jefferson Davis. In the doorway is the table on which the surrender of General Robert E. Lee was signed, April 1865 Photographer unknown

Burnt District (horses hitched to iron fence in foreground), April 1865, John Reekie, photographer

Ruins of the Exchange Bank (Main Street) with the facade nearly intact, April, 1865, Photographer unknown

Brevet Brigadier General John E. Milford of 3rd New York Infantry with his wife and Mr. and Mrs. William Allen on the porch of Mr. Allen's house at Richmond 1865, Matthew Brady, photographer

Barges with African Americans on the Canal; ruined buildings beyond, 1865, Alexander Gardner Photographer unknown

Graves of Confederate Soldiers in Oakwood Cemetery, with board markers, 1865, Photographer unknown

Group of Negroes ("Freedmen") by Canal, 1865, Alexander Gardner, photographer

Bridge over the Canal; barges beyond, April-June 1865, Alexander Gardner, photographer

Federal Soldiers in Front of City Hall, April 1865, Alexander Gardner, photographer

Capital Square, 1865, Alexander Gardner, photographer

Negro Women sitting on Rocks, Richmond, Virginia, 1865, Alexander Gardner, photographer

Christian Commission, Richmond, Virginia, April, 1865, photographer unknown

Judith White Brockenbrough McGuire, late 19th century,
photographer unknown

Constance Cary Harrison, Date and photographer unknown

Mary Tucker Magill, Date and photographer unknown

Phoebe Yates Pember, Date and photographer unknown

View of Richmond, Virginia, 1865, Matthew Brady, photographer

Two Women in Black, April, 1865, Alexander Gardner, photographer

Residence of Jefferson Davis (1201 East Clay Street), April-June, 1865, photographer unknown

St. Paul's Episcopal Church (Grace Street), April, 1865, John Reekie, photographer

Houses on Governor Street—April 1865, photographer unknown

St. John's Church and Graveyard from the street, April-June 1865,
photographer unknown

Ruined Buildings in the Burned District, April-June, 1865,
photographer unknown

General Edward O.C. Ord, wife and child at the Residence of Jefferson Davis. In the doorway is the table on which the surrender of General Robert E. Lee was signed. April 1865, photographer unknown

Burnt District (horses hitched to iron fence in foreground), April 1865, John Reekie, photographer

Ruins of the Exchange Bank (Main Street) with the facade nearly
intact, April, 1865, photographer unknown

Brevet Brigadier General John E. Milford of 3rd New York Infantry with his wife and Mr. and Mrs. William Allen. This picture was taken on the porch of Mr. Allen's house at Richmond, Virginia, 1865, Matthew Brady, photographer

Barges with African Americans on the Canal; ruined buildings
beyond, 1865, Alexander Gardner, photographer

Graves of Confederate Soldiers in Oakwood Cemetery, with board
markers, 1865, photographer unknown

Group of Negroes ("Freedmen") by Canal, April, 1865, photographer
unknown

Bridge over the Canal; Barges beyond, April-June 1865, Alexander
Gardner, photographer

Federal Soldiers in Front of City Hall, April 1865, Alexander Gardner, photographer

Capital Square, 1865, Alexander Gardner, photographer

Negro Women sitting on Rocks, Richmond, Virginia, 1865, Alexander
Gardner, photographer

Christian Commission, Richmond, Virginia, April, 1865,
photographer unknown

OVERVIEW

(ed: As we celebrate the sesquicentennial of the civil war, I thought that it would be interesting to include an overview of the war from the Richmonder's perspective at the Centennial mark. The following are excerpts from a speech given by C. Hobson Goddin, Vice Chairman of the Richmond Civil War Centennial Committee.)

. . . Richmond's reputation developed as a gay and fun-loving community. Its taverns and coffee-houses (like Lynch's, Mrs. Gilbert's, Bird-in-Hand and Eagle to name but a very few) were renowned far from the borders of the City. Their catholic stocks ranged from the rarest wines of Spain and Portugal to the rawest of local rums; their fares offered the best of imported delicacies garnished with fresh vegetables from the near-by farms of Hanover County.

Richmond was famed as one of the thespian centers of the new nation. Before the outbreak of The War, more than a dozen theatrical halls gave the devotee of the footlights his choice of programs from such stars as Jenny Lind (at $105.00 per seat), Edwin Booth and Joe Jefferson to earthy burlesque (at 25¢ per seat). But whether you chose the Marshall Theatre or Metropolitan Hall or thrilled to Old Blind Tom at the African Baptist Church, it was well to buy your ticket in advance should you wish to avoid S. R. 0. (Standing Room Only)

William Ellery Channing, Edgar Allan Poe and Albert Gallatin had placed their marks of cosmopolitan culture upon our people with indelibility. The visits of Marquis de Lafayette, Charles Dickens and William Makepeace Thackery had forever removed from us any cover of provincial isolationism. Indeed, Richmond could hold its own, socially or culturally, with New Orleans, New York and Charleston.

Also, Richmond was an important transportation center, with rail and steamer connections, north and south, east and west. The James River and Kanawha Canal was a vital water artery westward and was used throughout the War for the transfer of troops and supplies. . . .

With Secession on 17 April 1861, the Richmond City Council went to work. On 9 May 1861, a committee of the Council was appointed to wait on General R. E. Lee to ask his advice as to the expediency of taking steps to put this City in a state of defense, with Mayor Joseph Mayo furnishing the necessary labor from among the unemployed Negroes.

The City also resolved to purchase and make a gift of the home at the southeast corner of 12th and Clay Streets as an official residence for the President. $35,000 was authorized for this purpose but the Confederate Government decided that the purchase instead should be made by them in the name of all of the people of all of the states.

Early on the morning of 29 May 1861, Jefferson Davis arrived by train from Montgomery, Alabama, to establish Richmond as the Capital of the Confederacy. A great crowd was on hand—as Virginia had not long before seceded from the Union, which she had done so much to create, to cast her lot with her Southern neighbors.

Richmond in 1861 was one vast army camp—finely dressed military companies from the Southern States were assembling here—the cadets of V. M. I. under Jackson had arrived and were serving as instructors. Not to be thought of were the horrors of suffering and the grief of the war to be.

But the First Battle of Manassas (Bull Run) on 21 July 1861 soon brought an end to the glamorous side of war—'ere long the trains of the Virginia Central Railroad were bringing in the wounded from the battlefields. Ill-equipped to meet the demand for hospitals, the City was housing the sick and wounded in warehouses, even the parlors of private homes, where they were tenderly administered to by the women.

With the opening of the guns of the first major struggle for Richmond at Seven Pines (Fair Oaks) 31 May-1 June 1862, the citizens rushed to the hillsides and to the rooftops to view the repulse of the invader. Out of the next series of battles, known as the Seven Day battles, lives the heroic defense of this City.

But from many doorways waved the black symbol of death—the once quiet streets heard the continual passing of funeral processions to Hollywood and Oakwood Cemeteries. Richmond had changed from a pleasure-loving City to one of resolute men and women, determined to make any sacrifice for their cause.

On many occasions as the troops passed thru the City, ill-fed and poorly clothed, the citizens would have their own meals brought out on the sidewalk so that the soldiers might have a quick bite. The children would shower the men with flowers so that the ragged army would almost be in bloom from those stuck in the hats of the men and in the gun-barrels.

With the tightening of the blockade and the increase in population, prices went up—coffee was $4.00 per pound, tea $20.00, cloth and new fashions were rarities. It was not too long before old draperies were transformed into new dresses. A single hotel meal cost nine Confederate soldiers $600. It was said that formerly when a lady took her purse to market that she needed a basket to carry home her purchases; now she needed a basket for her money and a purse for her purchases. There were no rats or mice in the City—not even pigeons.

The gnawing of hunger was ever present. In April of 1863, there was a bread-riot in the market area. There was simply not enough food to go around and what there was the cost was so exorbitant in that many families were forced to sell their most cherished possessions to feed themselves. The citizens kept their faith, tightened their belts—and hoped.

In 1864, the Union forces again were before Richmond. But now the outcome was inevitable. The superiority of manpower and material of war was too much. Yet the City hung on desperately, until even Lee confessed that Richmond was a "millstone" around his neck for he knew that a siege would slowly strangle his Army.

By this time Richmond had become shabby in appearance. Houses needed painting and Sam Landrum's brushes were dry from the lack of paint. Roofs and fences required repair. To a city where a nail, or a needle, was a prized possession and where every sacrifice was for the men in the field, the people could endure.

Starvation parties became popular—music was furnished, but absolutely no food or drink was served except "the brown water of the James". The swollen population had reached well over 125,000.

There was always the fear of uprisings among the prisoners, who numbered at one time 13,000. And there was an added fear of slave insurrections—but they remained faithful thru out, "prayed for victory by the South and our suffering soldiers". Thousands of them worked on the defense fortifications around Richmond and their spade work is much in evidence today.

In April 1864, the prisoner of war exchanges were resumed and to the Capital Square came a thousand ragged and emaciated men. Picture families with all their meager food supplies roamed through the crowd looking hopefully for husbands, fathers, sons and kinsmen.

In May, there was yet another naval attack stopped at Drewry's Bluff. In June, there was heard the fearful bloody roar of cannon at Cold Harbor. In September, the Union forces almost broke thru Richmond's defenses at Fort Harrison. In October, Godfrey Weitzel's men were repulsed at the very edge of the last line defending the eastern front of the City.

On a quiet morning—Sunday 2 April—a messenger came up Ninth Street and moved swiftly down the aisle of Saint Paul's with a fateful message for President Davis. The City must be evacuated! Imagine the excitement and the distress of the people as they came out onto the sidewalk to discuss what could be done. Richmonders, so long accustomed to their successful defenses and with their faith in General Lee and his heroic army, could scarcely believe that Richmond, at last, had to be abandoned.

As the remaining troops of the Confederate Army left the City by Mayo's Bridge, General Dick Ewell's men began putting the torch to the cotton and tobacco warehouses, the arsenal and the powder magazines. Lawless elements began looting the commissaries and the stores. A half-starved population became a vast uncontrollable, leaderless mob. In such chaos no one could think of sleeping. The fires raged beyond control, munitions were blowing up—many took what scant belongings that they could gather and sought refuge in Capital Square to escape the flames. For hours, the City was without law and order. A pure state of anarchy existed!

Early the next morning and at the height of the blaze, in marched the Yankee forces. Up Main Street and onto Ninth and thru the entrance gates in front of the Square, they came. Down came the Confederate flag from the roof. Up went the flag of the United States of America—for the first time in four years . . . The Federal troops under set about to put out the fires, to restore law and order, to protect the women and weak and to issue food to the half-starved populace.

Gone was the heart of the business district, completely destroyed. The areas from the north side of Main Street to the James River, 8th thru 15th and from 4th thru 10th, south of Canal Street, were nothing but smoldering ruins and ashes—over 900 houses had been destroyed!

On Wednesday 5 April, President Abraham Lincoln visited Richmond for the first and last time as he was to be assassinated within a fortnight. He walked, slowly and bravely, with his little son Tad holding his hand, up Main Street, thence up Governor Street to Jefferson Davis' White House. Later he rode in an open carriage along Grace Street, viewing the shell of a city.

Just a few days later, mounted on his faithful Traveler, General R. E. Lee turned, rain-soaked, into Franklin Street—Home from Appomattox—Home after four years of war.

But from the ashes of defeat, Richmond has risen again to a place of prominence in the South and in the Nation. We pause in these Centennial Years to commemorate the valiant deeds and sacrifices of the men and the women of this City, the once proud Capital of the Confederacy, for their dedication to a cause in which they believed. [1]

LADIES

Leading Lady

Judith B. McGuire

Judith Brockenbrough McGuire was born in 1813 as the daughter of a Virginia Supreme Court Judge and married John P. McGuire in 1846. John was an Episcopalian minister and the founder of the Theological Seminary in Alexandria Virginia. Her father, William, studied at the College of William & Mary and was elected to represent Essex County in the Virginia House of Delegates in 1802.

They were forced to flee their home in Alexandria on May 24, 1861 and took refuge with various family members before deciding to settle in Richmond. The wartime economy and the loss of her husband's pastoral income forced them to both work. John became a clerk with the Post Office and a hospital chaplain. Judith McGuire was employed the Commissary Department with a salary of $125 per month. They moved several times while in Richmond, always searching for affordable and adequate living accommodations. Judith published her diary, *Diary of a Southern Refugee during the War*, in 1867. The diary had two editions in its first year alone and a third edition was published in 1889.

The McGuires never regained their antebellum prosperity. They were forced to accept her brother's offer to live with him after the fall of Richmond. John finally received a pastorate of several small churches in Essex County and they established a home there. He died in 1869. In the 1870s, Judith operated a school for boys. They never returned to Alexandria. Judith died in 1897.

Other Ladies

Myrta Lockett Avary

Myrta Lockett Avary was born in Halifax County in 1857 and raised in Mecklenburg County, Virgina. She moved to Atlanta after she married James Corbin Avary in 1884. In the 1890s, she moved to New York. She authored a *Virginia Girl in the Civil War* and *Dixie after the War* and was the editor of *A Diary from Dixie* as written by Mary Boykin Chesnut (1905). She died in 1949.

Fannie Taylor Dickinson

Fannie Taylor Dickinson was born in 1830 in Richmond, Virginia. She was the daughter of James A. Taylor, the minister of Leigh Street Baptist Church. In 1857, she married Rev. Alfred E. Dickinson who subsequently become the pastor of Leigh Street Baptist Church from 1865-1870. She chronicled the events surrounding the fall of Richmond. She died in 1879.

Constance Cary Harrison

Constance Cary Harrison was born in 1843 into an aristocratic planter family. They moved to Cumberland, Maryland, where her father was a newspaper editor. When he died in 1854, they moved to a plantation in Fairfax County, Virginia. During the war, she lived in Virginia and moved in the same social set as Varina Davis and Mary Boykin Chesnut. She became published in Southern magazines. After the war, she settled in New York City. Her writings included *Virginia Battle Scenes in '61* and *Reflections Gay and Grave*. She died in Washington, D.C. in 1920.

Mary Tucker Magill

Mary Tucker Magill was born in 1830. She was the daughter of Ann Evelina Tucker, the daughter of U.S. Congressman, Virginia jurist and a university professor Dr. Alfred T. Magill and the granddaughter of William & Mary law professor Henry St George Tucker (1780-1848). Mary spent her childhood in Jefferson County, Virginia, and received her education in Richmond and went to University of Virginia, where her father was a professor of medicine. In 1848, Magill became one of the first instructors of the Valley Female Seminary. She wrote several books, including *Women: Or Chronicles of the Late War* (1871). She died in 1899.

Phoebe Yates Pember

Phoebe Yates Levy was born in 1823 and was raised in Charleston, South Carolina in a socially prominent Jewish family. She was married to Bostonian Thomas Pember who died shortly after their marriage. Phoebe was appointed to serve as the Warden of Richmond Chimborazo Hospital in December, 1862. She assumed the responsibility at the age 39 and eventually over 15,000 patients came under her care until the Confederate surrender in April, 1865. After the war, she wrote her memoirs, *A Southern Woman's Story: Life in Confederate Richmond (1879)*. She died in 1913.

Sallie Brock Putnam

Sallie Brock Putnam was born in Madison Courthouse, Virginia, in 1845. She was born into a privileged class. She lived in Richmond with her mother, and, in 1867, after her mother died, she moved to New York to pursue a literary career. She published *Richmond during the War; Four Years of Personal Observation* upon her arrival in New York. She married Rev. Richard Putnam in 1883 and lived in Brooklyn, New York until she died in 1911.

CHAPTER ONE
1861—LEAVING HOME

". . . With heavy heart I packed trunks and boxes, as many as our little carriage would hold." —Judith McGuire

Judith McGuire Diary

Alexandria, Virginia. At home, May 4, 1861 . . . Can it be that our country is to be on to the horrors of civil war? I pray, oh how fervently do I pray, that our Heavens yet avert it. I shut my eyes and hold my breath when the thought of what may come obtrudes itself; and yet I cannot believe it. It will, I know the breach will be healed with an effusion of blood. The taking of Sumter without bloodshed has somewhat soothed my fears., though I am told by those who are wiser than I, that men must fall on both sides by the score, by the hundred, and even by the thousand. But it is not my habit to look on the dark side, so I try hard to employ myself, and hope for the best.

To-day the house seems so deserted, that I feel more sad than usual, for on this morning we took leave of our whole household. Mr.—and myself are now the sole occupants of the house, which usually teems with life. I go from room to room, looking first at one thing and then another, so full of sad associations. The closed piano, the locked bookcase, the nicely-arranged tables, the formally-placed chairs, ottomans and sofas in the parlor! Oh for someone to put them out of order! And then the dinner-table, which has always been so well surrounded, so social so cheerful, looked so cheerless to-day, as we seated ourselves one at the head, the other at the foot, with one friend,—but one—at the side. I could scarcely restrain my tears, and for the presence of that one friend, I believed that I should have cried outright. After dinner, I did not mean to do it, but I could not help going into the girl's room and then into C.'s. I heard my own footsteps so plainly that I was startled by the absences of all other sounds. There the furniture looked so quiet, the beds so fixed and smooth, the wardrobes and bureau so tightly locked, and the whole so lifeless! But the writing-desks, work-boxes, and the numberless things so familiar to my eyes! Where were they? I paused and asked myself what it all meant. Why did we think it necessary to send off all that was so dear to us from our own home? I threw open the shutters, and the answer came at once, so mournfully! I heard distantly the drums beating in Washington. The evening was so still that I seemed to hear nothing else. As I looked at the Capitol in the distance, I could scarcely believe my senses. That Capitol of which I had always been so proud. Can it be possible that it is no longer *our* Capitol? And are our countrymen, under its very eaves, making mighty preparation to drain our hearts' blood? And must this Union, which I was taught to revere, be rent asunder? Once I thought such a suggestion sacrilege; but now that it is dismembered, I trust it may never, never be reunited. We must be a separate people—our nationality must be different, to insure lasting peace and good-will. Why cannot we part in peace?

May 10 . . . War seems inevitable, and, while I am trying to employ the passing hour, a cloud still hangs over us and all that surrounds us. For a long time, our society was so completely broken up, the ladies of Alexandria and all the surrounding country were busily employed sewing for our soldiers. Shirts, pants, jackets and beds, all of the heaviest material, have been made by the most delicate fingers. All ages, all conditions, meet now on one common platform. We must all work for our country. Our soldiers must be equipped. Our parlor was the rendezvous for our neighborhood, and our sewing-machine was in requisition for weeks. Scissors and needles were plied by all. The daily scene was most animated. The fires of our enthusiasm and patriotism were burning all the while to a degree which might have been consuming, but that our tongues served as safety valves. . . . We are very weak in resources, but strong in stout hearts, zeal for the cause, and enthusiastic devotion to our beloved South;

and while men are making a free-will offering of their life's blood on the altar of their country, women must not be idle. We must do what we can for the comfort of our brave men. We must sew for them, knit for them, nurse the sick, keep up the fainthearted, and give them a word of encouragement in season and out of seasons. . . .

. . . Busy life has departed from our midst. We found Mrs.—packing up valuables. I have been doing the same; but after they are packed, where are they to be sent? Silver may be buried, but what is to be done with books, pictures, etc.? We have determined if we are obliged to go from home, to leave everything in the care of the servants. They have promised to be faithful, and I believe they will be; but my hope becomes stronger and stronger that we may remain here, or may soon return if we go away.

May 15—Busy every moment of time packing up, that our furniture may be safely put away in case of a sudden removal. The parlor furniture has been rolled into the laboratory, and covered, to keep it from injury; the books are packed up; the pictures are put away with care; house linen locked up, and all other things made as secure as possible. We do not hope to remove many things but to prevent their ruin. We are constantly told that a large army would do great injury if quartered near us; therefore we want to put things out of the reach of the soldiers, for I have no idea that officers would allow them to break locks, or that they would allow our furniture to be interfered with. We have a most unsettling feeling—with carpets up, curtains down, and the rooms without furniture; but a constant excitement, and expectation of we know not what, supplants all other feelings. . . . Let States, like individuals, be independent—be something or nothing. I believe that the very best people of both States are with us, but held back by stern necessity. Oh that they could burst the bonds that bind them, and speak and act like freemen! The Lord reigneth; to Him we can only turn, and humbly pray that He may see fit to say to the troubled waves. "Peace, be still!" We sit at our windows, and see the bosom of our own Potomac covered with sails of vessels employed by the enemies of our peace. I often wish myself far away, that I, at least, might not *see* these things. The newspapers are filled with the boastings of the North, and yet I cannot feel alarmed. My woman's heart does not quail, even though they come, as they so loudly threaten, as an avalanche to overwhelm us. Such is my abiding faith in the justice of our cause, that I have no shadow of doubt of our success.

21ˢᵗ . . . Day after to-morrow the vote of Virginia on secession will be taken, and I, who so dearly loved this Union, who from my cradle was taught to revere it, now most earnestly hope that the voice of Virginia may give no uncertain sound; that she may leave it with a shout. I am thankful that she did not take so important a step hastily, but that she set an example of patience and long-suffering, and made an earnest effort to maintain peace; but all her efforts have been rejected with scorn, and she has been required to give her quota of men to fight and destroy her brethren of the South, I trust that she may now speak decidedly.

Fairfax C.H. May 25—The day of suspense is at an end. Alexandria and its environs, including, I greatly fear, our home are in the hands of the enemy. Yesterday morning, at an early hour, as I was in my pantry, putting up refreshments for the barracks preparatory to a ride to Alexandria, the door was suddenly thrown open by a servant, looking wild with excitement, exclaiming, "Oh, madam, do you know?" "Know what, Henry?" "Alexandria is filled with Yankees." "Are you sure, Henry?" said I, trembling in every limb. "Sure, madam! I saw them myself. Before I got up, I heard soldiers rushing by the door; went out, and saw our men going to the cars." "Did they get off?" I asked, afraid to hear the answer. "Oh, yes, the cars went off full of them, and some marched out; and then I went to King Street, and saw such crowds of Yankees coming in! They came down the turnpike, and some came down the river; and presently I heard such noise and confusion, and they said they were fighting, so I can home as fast as I could.

. . . With heavy heart I packed trunks and boxes, as many as our little carriage would hold; had packing boxes fixed in my room for the purpose of bringing off valuables of various sorts, when I go down on Monday; locked up everything; gave the keys to the cook, enjoining upon the servants to take care of the cows, "Old Rock," the garden, the flowers, and last, but not the least, J—'s splendid Newfoundland. Poor dog, as we got into the carriage how I did long to take him! When we took leave of the servants they looked sorrowful, and we felt so. I promised them to return to-day, but Mr.—was so sick this morning that I could not leave him, and have deferred to it until day after to-morrow. Mr.—said, as he looked out upon the green lawn just before we set off, that he thought he had never seen the place so attractive; and as we drove off the bright flowers we had planted seemed in full glory; every flower bed seemed to glow with the "Giant of Battles" and other brilliant roses. In bitterness of heart I exclaimed "Why must we leave thee, Paradise!" and for the first time my tears streamed. . . . When we got to Bailey's Cross Roads, Mr.—said to me that we were obligated to leave our home, and we have *no right* to any other, it makes not the slightest difference which road we take—we might as well drive to the right hand as to the left—nothing remains to us but the barren, beaten track. It was a sorrowful thought; but we have kind relations and friends whose doors are open to us, and we hope to get home again before very long. The South did not bring on the war, and I believe God will provide for the homeless.

May 29—I cannot get over my disappointment—I am not to return home! The wagon was engaged. . . . Ah, how many Northerners—perhaps the very men who have come to despoil these homes, to kill our husbands, son and brothers, to destroy our peace—have been partakers of the warmhearted hospitality so freely offered by our people! The parlors and dining rooms so ignominiously searched, how often have they been opened, and the best cheer which the houses could afford set forth for them! I do most earnestly hope that no Northern gentlemen, above all, no Christian gentlemen, will engage in this wicked war of invasion. It makes my blood boil when I remember that our private rooms, our chambers, our very sanctums, are thrown open to a ruthless soldiery. . . .

(ed: The McGuires were starting a long journey that would last until 1865. Forced to abandon their home, they fled with only a limited amount of household goods and clothing, not knowing when, if ever, they would see their beloved home again. The upcoming war's duration and intensity is beyond their wildest expectations.

Collectively, this displaced and migrant group was called "refugees". They were buffeted by rumors of questionable reliability. Emotions ran high and even wild rumors had apparent credibility. They struggled with the decision of whether it was safer to move or to stay and protect their homes. In many cases, women were suddenly forced to make a decision of this nature alone since the men were being mobilized into the Confederate army. In their haste to escape imminent enemy invasion, they lacked proper preparation or plans as to where to go and for how long. They were financially ill-equipped for this migrant life and this caused an increasing burden on relatives and communities. They became preoccupied with securing the basic necessities of life and finding temporary housing from family and friends. After exhausting the hospitality of relatives, they migrated to cities that offered employment opportunities, safety, police protection and a variety of living arrangements. However, as their numbers increased, the attitudes of sympathy waned as the scarcity of food, shelter and jobs increased. The Richmond Examiner described the refugees as "vultures preying on the community." The newspaper had supported benevolence to the refugees early in the war.

CHAPTER TWO

JUST VISITING

"Oh, that they would now consent to leave our soil, and return to their homes." —Judith McGuire

Judith Maguire's Diary Continues

Chantilly June 6 . . . Letters from Richmond are very cheering. It is one great barracks. Troops are assembling there from every part of the Confederacy, all determined to do their duty. Ladies assemble daily, by hundreds, at various churches, for the purpose of sewing for the soldiers. They are fitting out company after company. The large stuccoed house at the corner of Clay and Twelfth streets, so long occupied by Dr. John Brockenbrough, has been purchased as a residence for the President.

Clark County for the summer,

The Briars June 12 . . . After driving some miles over the delightful turnpike, we found ourselves at this door, receiving the warm-hearted welcome of the kindest of relatives and the most pleasant of hosts. Our daughters were here before us, all well, and full of questions about "home". This is all very delightful when we fancy ourselves making a *voluntary* visit to this family, as in days gone by, to return home when the visit is over, hoping to see our friends by our own fireside; but the reality is before us that we were forced from home and can only return when it pleases our enemy to open the way for us, or when our men have forced them away at the point of

7

the bayonet, then does our future seem shadowy, doubtful and dreary, and then we feel that our situation is indeed sorrowful. But these feelings must not be indulged; many are already in our situation, how many more are there who may have to follow our example! Having no houses to provide for, we must be up and doing for our country; idleness does not become us now—there is too much to be done; we must work on, work ever, and let our country's weal be our being's end and aim.

Winchester, July 19—This day is perhaps the most anxious of my life. It is believed that a battle is going on at or near Manassas. Our large household is in a state of feverish anxiety; but we cannot talk of it. . . .

July 20— . . . The fight on Thursday lasted several hours; our loss was fifteen killed, about forty wounded; in all about eighty to eighty-five missing. It is believed that at least 900 of the enemy were left on the field; 150 of their slightly wounded have been sent to Richmond as prisoners. The severely wounded are in the hands of our surgeons at Manassas.

Monday—We hear nothing from Manassas at all reliable. Men are passing through the neighborhood giving contradictory reports. They are evidently deserters. They only concur in one statement—that there was a battle yesterday.

(ed: *Throughout the war, the citizens found it difficult to receive reliable reports as to the progress of the war in general and battle information in particular. The main source of information was the soldiers who were returning to rest or to recover from their wounds.*)

Tuesday—The victory is ours! The enemy was routed! The Lord be praised for this great victory.

Evening . . . We certainly routed the enemy, and already wonderful stories are told of the pursuit. We shall hear all from time to time. It is enough for us now to know that their great expectations are disappointed, and that we have gloriously gained our point. Oh, that they would now consent to leave our soil, and return to their homes! If I know my own heart, I do not desire vengeance upon then, but only that they leave us in peace, to be forever and forever a separate people. It is true that we have slaughtered them, and whipped them, and driven them from our land, but they are people of such indomitable perseverance, that I am afraid that they will come again, perhaps in greater force. The final result I do not fear; but I do dread the butchery of our young men.

Constance Cary Harrison's Recollections

7/28/61—A week after the first battle of Manassas I rode on horseback with a party over the field, between hill-sides piled with hecatombs of dead horses and scattered with hasty graves. The trees and undergrowth were broken and bullet-riddled. The grass between the scars of upturned earth was green as if it had known no baptism of fire and blood, and little wild flowers had already begun to bloom again, but for obvious reasons we could take but a passing glimpse. I saw a ghastly semblance of a hand protruding at one spot, and thought of it when I stood in the crypt of the Pantheon, in Paris, by the gloomy tomb of Rousseau, where a skeleton hand holds up from within the bronze coffin lid of the French philosopher and epoch-maker. . . . [2]

Judith McGuire's Diary Continue

July 30 . . . There seems to be no probability of our getting home and, if we cannot, what then? What will become of our furniture, and all our comforts, books, pictures, etc.! But these things are too sad to dwell on.

October 2d . . . The number of refugees increases fearfully as our army falls back; for though many persons, still surrounded by all the comforts of home, ask why they do not stay, and protect their property, my only answer is, "How can they?' In many instances defenseless women and children are left without the means of subsistence; their crops destroyed; their business suspended; their servants gone; their horses and other stock taken off; their houses liable at any hour of the day or night to be entered and desecrated by a lawless soldiery. How can they remain without the present means of support, and nothing in prospect? The enemy will dole them out rations, it is said, if they take the oath! But who so base as to do that? Can southern women sell her birthright for a mess of pottage? Would she not be unworthy of the husband, the son, the brother who is now offering himself a willing sacrifice on the alter of his country? And our old men, the hoary-headed fathers of heroic sons, can they bear the insults, the taunting of an invading army? Can they see the spot of earth which they have perhaps inherited from their fathers covered with the tents of the enemy; their houses used as head-quarters by officers, while they and their families are forced into the poorest accommodations. . . . ancestral trees laid low, to make room for fortifications, thrown across their grounds, from which cannon will point to the very heart of their loved South? How can the venerable gentlemen of the land stay at home and bear such things? . . .

Thursday, 24th—An account reached us to-day of a severe fight last Monday (21st), at Leesburg—a Manassas fight in a small way . . .

[November] 15th—This was fast-day—national fast proclaimed by our President. I trust that every church in the Confederacy was well filled with heart-worshippers. . . .

Constance Cary Harrison's Recollections Continue

In the autumn (1861), when my cousins had gone to Albemarle to visit relatives, we three had the honor of being asked by the committee of Congress to make the first battle-flags of the Confederacy after the design finally decided on by them. It is generally stated by historians that these flags were constructed from our own dresses, but it is certain we possessed no wearing apparel in the flamboyant hues of poppy red and vivid dark blue required. We had a great search for materials. I had to content myself with a poor quality of red silk for the field of mine, necessitating an interlining, which I regretted. I have always been sorry we did not keep the model sketches, with directions, assigned to us by the committee which decided the matter, and delivered by Major A. D. Banks. Our work done, a golden fringe sewed around each flag (and, in my case, my name embroidered upon it in golden letters), we were at liberty to present them as head-quarters banners to our favorite generals. Miss Hetty Cary, having first choice, sent hers to General Joseph E. Johnston, Miss Jennie Cary's went to General Beauregard—serving to drape the coffin of Beauregard and of Jefferson Davis—and mine to General Earl Van Dorn, a dashing cavalry leader, for whom was then predicted great fame and success. I had never seen Van Dorn, and was rather alarmed at my temerity in selecting him, but I knew his aide-de-camp, Captain Durant da Ponté, grandson of the librettist of "Don Giovanni," and himself a charming poet. Through Captain da Ponté, I was emboldened to send off my flag, with the following note. In those days, as I have shown, we were in favor of the flowery style of expressing high sentiment. I transcribe the correspondence from a newspaper clipping of the period:

CULPEPER COURT HOUSE, VA.,
Nov. 10, 1861

Will General Van Dorn honor me by accepting a flag which I have taken great pleasure in making, and now send with an earnest prayer that the work of my hand may hold its place near him as he goes out to a glorious struggle—and, God willing, may one day wave over the re-captured batteries of my home near the down-trodden Alexandria?

I am, very respectfully, Genl. Van Dorn's obedient servant,

Constance Cary

ARMY OF THE POTOMAC, MANASSAS,
Nov. 12, 1861.

To Miss Constance Cary, CULPEPER C. H.

Dear Lady:

The beautiful flag made by your hands and presented to me with the prayer that it should be borne by my side in the impending struggle for the existence of our country, is an appeal to me as a soldier as alluring as the promises of glory; but when you express the hope, in addition, that it may one day wave over the re-captured city of your nativity, your appeal becomes a supplication so beautiful and holy that I were craven-spirited indeed, not to respond to it with all the ability that God has given me. Be assured, dear young lady, that it shall wave over your home if Heaven smiles upon our cause, and I live, and that there shall be written upon it by the side of your name which it now bears, 'Victory, Honor and Independence.'

In the meantime, I shall hope that you may be as happy as you, who have the soul thus to cheer the soldier on to noble deeds and to victory—should be, and that the flowers wont to bloom by your window, may bloom as sweetly for you next May, as they ever did, to welcome you home again.

Very truly and respectfully, dear lady, I am your humble and obedient servant.

Earl Van Dorn, Major-General, P. A. C. S.

Captain da Ponté told me that, when the flag arrived at Van Dorn's head-quarters and was adopted into the division, a young officer sprang up, unsheathed his sword, and held it hilt downward upon the table, while one after the other of his comrades clasped the blade; when all swore a knightly oath to make good the giver's petition, after which they drank to the flag and to her. [3]

CHAPTER THREE

1862—ON TO RICHMOND!

"The city is overrun with members of Congress, government officers, office-seekers and strangers generally."—Judith McGuire

Judith McQuire's Diary Continues

Westwood, Hanover County, January 20, 1862—I pass over the sad leave-taking of our kind friends in Clark and Winchester. It was very sad, because we knew not when and under what circumstances we might meet again. We left Winchester, in the stage, at ten o'clock at night, on the 24th of December. . . .

Richmond, February 5.—For two weeks my diary has been a closed book. After another week at W., we went to the Presbyterian Parsonage to join the refugee family who had gathered within its walls. They had made themselves comfortable and it had a *home-like* appearance. After remaining there a day or two, Mr.—received a letter, announcing his appointment to a clerkship in the Post-Office Department. The pleasure and gratitude with it is received is only commensurate with the necessity which made him apply for it. It seems a strange state of things which induces a man, who has ministered and served the alter for thirty-six years, to accept joyfully a situation purely secular, for the purposes of making his living; but no chaplaincy could be obtained except on the field, which would neither suit his health, his age, nor his circumstances. His salary will pay his board and mine in Richmond, and the girls will stay in the country until they or I can obtain writing from the Government—note-signing from Mr. Memminger or something else. We are spending a few days with our niece, Mrs. H.A.C. until we can find board. . . .

The city is overrun with members of Congress, Government officers, office-seekers, and strangers generally. Main Street is crowded as Broadway, New York; it is said that every boarding-house is full.

February 6—Spent this day in walking from one boarding-house to another, and have returned fatigued and hopeless. I do not believe that there is a vacant spot in the city. A friend, who considers herself *nicely* fixed, is in an uncarpeted room, and so poorly furnished, that, besides her trunk, she has only her washstand drawer in which to deposit her goods and chattels; and yet she amuses herself at it, and seems never to regret her handsomely furnished chamber in Alexandria.

7th—Walking all day, with no better success. "No vacant room." is the universal answer. I returned at dinner-time, wearied in mind and body. I have been cheered by suggestions that perhaps Mrs.___, with a large family and small income, may take boarders; or Mrs.—, with a large house and small family, may do the same.

8th—I have called on the two ladies mentioned above. The lady with the small income has filled her rooms, and wishes she had more to fill. She of the large house and small family had "never dreamed of taking boarders," was "surprised that such a thing was suggested," looked cold and lofty, and meant me to *feel* that she was far too rich for that. I bowed myself out, feeling not a little scornful of such airs, particularly as I remembered the time when she was not quite so grand. I went on my way speculating on turning of the wheel of fortune, until I reached the house of an old acquaintance, and rang her bell, hoping that she may take in wanderers. This I did not venture to suggest, but told her my story in pitiful tones. She was all sympathy, and would be glad to take us it, but for the reserve of a bachelor brother to whom the house belonged. She appreciated the situation, and advised me to call on Mrs.____ on ____ Street. Nothing daunted from past experience, I bent my steps to ____ Street and soon explained my object to Mrs.—. She had vacant rooms until two days ago, but a relative had taken both. Though she spoke positively, she looked doubtful, and I thought I saw indecision in the expression of her mouth. I ventured to expostulate: "perhaps the lady might be induced to give up one room." She hesitated and gave me an inquiring look. I told her my history. "An Episcopal minister." She exclaimed: "I'm an Episcopalian, and would be delighted to have a minister in the house. Do you think that he would have prayers for us sometimes?" "Oh, certainly, it would gratify him very much." "Well, the lady is not at home to-day, but when she comes I will try to persuade her to do it. Call on Monday." I thanked her and was walking out, when she called me back, saying, "You will not expect a constant fire in the parlor, will you?" "Oh, no; I can take my visitors to my own room." . . . I returned very much pleased and received the congratulations of my friends, who are taking much interest in our welfare.

Monday night . . . The lady on _____ Street has disappointed me. She met me with a radiant smile when I went to see her this evening, saying, "She agrees; she must, however, remove the wardrobe and bureau, as she wants them for herself; but there's a closet in the room, which will answer for a wardrobe, and I reckon that a table with glass on it will do for a bureau."

"Oh, yes; only give me a good bed, some chairs and a washstand, and I can get along very well. Can I see the room?" "Yes; it is a back-room in the third story, but I reckon that you won't mind that." My heart did sink a little at that communication, when I remembered Mr.—'s long walks from Bank Street; but there was no alternative, and I followed her up the steps. Great was my relief to find a large airy room, neatly carpeted and pleasant in all respects. "This will do," said I; "take the wardrobe and bureau out, and put a table in, and I shall be very well satisfied." "I have a small table," she replied, "but no glass; you will have to buy that." "Very well, I will do that. But you have not yet told me your terms." "Will you keep a fire?" "Oh, certainly, in my room." "Then my charge is _____." I stood aghast. "My dear madam," said I, "that is twenty dollars more than the usual price, and three dollars less than our whole salary per month." "Well; I can't take a cent less; other people take less because they want to fill their rooms, but I was only going to take you for accommodation; and I can fill my rooms at any time." Now the lines of her face were not undecided. I turned, and as I walked up the already lighted streets of my native city, feeling forlorn and houseless, and hope I was not envious. . . .

13th—Notwithstanding the rain this morning, I renewed my pursuit after lodgings. With over-shoes, cloak and umbrella, I defied the storm, and went over to Grace Street, to an old friend who sometimes takes boarders. Her house was full but with much interest she entered into my feelings, and advised me to go to Mr. L., who, his large school having declined, was filling his rooms with boarders. His wife was the daughter of a friend, and might find a nook for us. I thought of the "Hare and many friends," and bent my steps through the storm to the desired haven. To my surprise, Mrs. L. said we could get a room; it is small but comfortable, the terms suit our limited means, and we will go as soon as they let us know that they are ready for us.

Wednesday, 19th—We are now in our own comfortable little room on Grace Street and have quite a home-like feeling. . . .

We have just been drawn to the window by sad strains of martial music. The bodies of Captains Wise and Coles were brought by cars, under special escort. The military met them, and in the dark, cold night, it was melancholy to see the procession by lamplight, as it passed slowly down the street.

February 22—To-day I had hoped to see our President inaugurated, but the rains fall in torrents, and I cannot go. So many persons are disappointed, but we are comforted by knowing that the inauguration will take place, and that the reins of our government will continue to be in strong hands. . . . Our people are depressed by our recent disasters, but our soldiers are encouraged by the bravery and endurance of the troops at Donelson. It fell but not until human nature yielded from exhaustion. . . .

Our neighbor in the next room had two sons in that dreadful fight. Do they survive? Poor old lady! She can hear nothing from them; the telegraphic wires in Tennessee are cut and mail communication very uncertain. It is so sad to see that mother and sister quietly pursing their avocations, not knowing, the former says, whether she is not the second time widowed; for on those sons depend not only her comfort, but her means of subsistence, and that fair young girl, always accustomed to perfect ease, is now, with her old mother boarding—confined to one room, using her taste and ingenuity, making and altering bonnets, for her many acquaintances, that her mother may be supplied with the little luxuries to which she has always been accustomed, and which, her child says, "mother must have." . . .

(ed: With limited war news, each person was forced to interpret the events of the war. The loss of Forts Henry and Donelson resulted in the Confederates abandoning major areas in Kentucky and Tennessee. In addition, the Battle of Shiloh resulted in many casualties, and hopes of a short war with a Confederate victory waned. The true appreciation of the cost of war in terms of wounded and dead was beginning to be felt.)

7th—Just returned from the hospital. Several severe cases of typhoid fever require constant attention. . . . Some of them are very fond of hearing the Bible read; and I am yet to see the first soldier who has not received with apparent interest any proposition of being read to from the Bible . . .

March 11th—Yesterday we heard good news from the mouth of the James River. The Ship "Virginia" formerly the Merrimac, having been completely incased with iron, steamed into Hampton Roads, ran into the Federal vessel Cumberland, and then destroyed the Congress, and ran the Minnesota ashore. Others were damaged. We have heard nothing further; but this is glory enough for one day, for which we will thank God and take courage.

(ed: The Congress and the Minnesota were also Federal vessels.)

24th—Our people continue to make every effort to repel the foe, who, like the locusts of Egypt, overrun our land, carrying the bitterest enmity and desolation wherever they go. Troops are passing though Richmond on their way to Goldsborough, N. C. where it is said that Burnside is expected to meet them. Everybody is busy in supplying their wants as they pass through. On Sunday, just as the girls of one of the large seminaries were about to seat themselves at table, the principal of the school came in: "Young ladies," said he, "several extra trains have arrived unexpectedly, filled with troops. The committee appointed to attend them are total unprepared. What can we do to help our hungry soldiers?" "Give them our dinner," cried every young voice at once. In five minutes baskets were filled and the table was cleared. When the girls reached the cars, the street was thronged with ladies, gentlemen, servants, bearing waiters, dishes, trays, baskets filled with meats, bread, vegetables, etc. Every table in Richmond seemed to have sent its dinner to Broad Street, and our dear, dusty, hungry gray coats dined to their hearts' content, filled their haversacks, shouted "Richmond forever!" and went on their way rejoicing.

[April] 10th—Spent yesterday in the hospital by the bedside of Nathan Newton, our little Alabamian. I closed his eyes last night at ten o'clock, after an illness of six weeks. His body, by his own request, will be sent to his mother. Poor little boy! He was but fifteen, and should never left his home. It was sad to pack his knapsack, with his little gray suit, and colored shirts, so neatly stitched by his poor mother, of whom he so often spoke, calling to us in delirium, "Mother, mother." "Oh mother, come here." He so often called me mother, that I said to him one day, when his mind was clear, "Nathan, do I look like your mother?" "No, ma'am, not a bit; nobody is like my mother. . . ."

11th—The "Virginia" went out again to-day. The Federal Monitor would not meet her, but ran to Fortress Monroe, either for protection, or to tempt her under the heavy guns of the fortress; but she contented herself by taking three brigs and one schooner, and carrying them to Norfolk, with their cargoes. Soldiers are constantly passing through town. Everything seems to be in preparation for the great battle which is anticipated on the Peninsula. . . .

15th—A panic prevails lest the enemy should get to Richmond. Many persons are leaving town. I can't believe that they will get here, though it seems to be their end and aim. My mind is much perturbed; we can only go on doing our duty, as quietly as we can.

21st—The ladies are now engaged making sand-bags for the fortifications at Yorktown; every lecture-room in town crowded with them, sewing busily, hopefully, prayerfully. Thousands are wanted. No battle, but heavy skirmishing at Yorktown. . . . What does it all portend? We are intensively anxious; our conversation, while busily sewing at St. Paul's Lecture-Room, is only of war. We hear of so many horrors committed by the enemy in the Valley—houses searched and robbed, horses taken, sheep, cattle, etc. killed and carried off, servants deserting their homes, *churches desecrated!*

27th—The country is shrouded in gloom because of the fall of New Orleans! . . . I met two young Kentuckians tonight who had come out from their homes, leaving family and fortunes behind to help the South. After many difficulties, running the blockade across the Potomac, they reached Richmond yesterday, just as the news of the fall of New Orleans had overwhelmed the city. They are dreadfully disappointed by the tone of the persons they have met. They came burning with enthusiasm; and anything like depression is a shock to their excited feelings. One said to me that he thought he should return at once, as he had left every thing which made home desirable to help Virginia, and found her ready to give up. All the blood in my system boiled in an instant. "Where, sir," said I, "have you seen Virginians ready to give up their cause?" "Why," he replied. "I have been lounging about the Exchange all day, and have heard the sentiments of the people." "Lounging about the Exchange!" "And do you suppose that Virginians worthy of the name are now seen lounging about the Exchange? There you see the idlers and shirkers of the whole Southern army. No true man under forty-five is to be found there. Virginia, sir, is in the camp. Go there, and find the true men of the South. There they have been for one year, bearing the hardships, and offering their lives, and losing life and limb for the South; it is mournful to say how many! There you will find the chivalry of the South; and if Virginia does not receive you with the shout of enthusiasm which you anticipated, it is because the fire burns steadily and deeply; the surface blaze has long passed away. . . .

May 2d.—One young friend, J.S.M., is here, very ill; I am assisting to nurse him. I feel most anxious about him; he and his four brothers are nobly defending their country. They have strong motives, personal as well as patriotic. Their venerable father and mother, and two young sisters continue to be homeless. Their house has been burnt to the ground by Federal soldiers—furniture, clothing, important papers, all consumed. Sad as this story is, it is the history of so many families that it has ceased to call forth remark.

3d—It is distressing to see how many persons are leaving Richmond, apprehending that it is in danger, but it will not—I know it will not—fall.

It is said that the President does not fear; he will send his family away, because he thinks it is better for men, in whom the country's weal is so dependent, to be free from private anxiety. . . .

7th—Our 'peaceful' Sabbath was one of fearful strife at Williamsburg. We met and whipped the enemy. Oh, that we could drive them from our land forever! Much blood has been spilt on both sides; . . . two gentlemen came in, announcing heavy firing on the river. We had been painfully conscious of the firing before, but remembering the Drewry's Bluff was considered impregnable, I felt much more anxious about the patient than about the enemy. The gentlemen were panic-stricken, and one of them seemed to think that sunrise would find gun-boats at Rocketts. Not believing it possible, I felt no alarm, but the apprehensions of others made me nervous and unhappy. At daybreak I saw loads of furniture passing by, showing people were taking off their valuables.

12th— . . . Two hours ago, we heard of the destruction of the "Virginia" by our own people. It is a dreadful shock to the community. We can only hope that it was wisely done. Poor Norfolk must be given up. I can write no more today.

13th—General Jackson is doing so gloriously in the Valley that we must not let the fate of the "Virginia" depress us too much. . . .

29th—No official accounts from "Stonewall" and his glorious army, but private accounts are most cheering. In the meantime, the hospitals in and around Richmond are being cleared, aired, etc., preparatory to the anticipated battles. Oh, it is sickening to know that these precautions are necessary! Every man who is able has gone to his regiment. Country people are sending in all manner of things—shirts, drawers, socks, etc., hams, flour, fresh vegetables, fruits, preserves—for the sick and wounded. It is wonderful how these things can be spared. I suppose, if the truth be known, that they cannot be spared, except every man and women is ready to give up every article which is not absolutely necessary; and I dare say that gentlemen's wardrobes, which were wont to be numbered by dozens, are now reduced to couples.

It is said that General Johnston, by an admirable series of maneuvers, is managing to retreat from Williamsburg, all the time concealing the comparative weakness of his troops, and is retarding the advance of the enemy, until troops from other points can be concentrated here.

31st—The booming of cannon, at no very distant point, thrills us with apprehension. We know that a battle is going on. God help us! Now let every heart be raised to the God of battles.

Night—We have possession of the camp—the enemy's camp. The place is seven miles from Richmond. General Lee is ordered to take General Johnston's place. The fight may be renewed tomorrow.

Constance Cary Harrison's Reflections Continue

And now we come to the 31st of May, 1862, when the eyes of the whole continent turned to Richmond. On that day Johnston assaulted the Federals who had been advanced to Seven Pines. In face of recent reverses, we in Richmond had begun to feel like the prisoner of the Inquisition in Poe's story, cast into a dungeon of slowly contracting walls. With the sound of guns, therefore, in the direction of Seven Pines, every heart leaped as if deliverance were at hand. And yet there was no joy in the wild pulsation, since those to whom we looked for succor were our own flesh and blood, barring the way to a foe of superior numbers, abundantly provided, as we were not, with all the equipments of modern warfare, and backed by a mighty nation as determined as ourselves to win. Hardly a family in the town whose father, son, or brother was not part and parcel of the defending army.

When on the afternoon of the 31st it became known that the engagement had begun, the women of Richmond were still going about their daily vocations quietly, giving no sign of the inward anguish of apprehension. There was enough to do now in preparation for the wounded; yet, as events proved, all that was done was not enough by half. Night brought a lull in the cannonading. People lay down dressed upon beds, but not to sleep, while the weary soldiers slept upon their arms. Early next morning the whole town was on the street. Ambulances, litters, carts, every vehicle that the city could produce, went and came with a ghastly burden; those who could walk limped painfully home, in some cases so black with gunpowder they passed unrecognized. Women with pallid faces flitted bareheaded through the streets searching for their dead or wounded. The churches were thrown open, many people visiting them for a sad communion service or brief time of prayer; the lecture-rooms of various places of worship were crowded with ladies volunteering to sew, as fast as fingers could fly, the rough beds called for by the surgeons. Men too old or infirm to fight went on horseback or afoot to meet the returning ambulances, and in some cases served as escort to their own dying sons. By afternoon of the day following the battle, the streets were one vast hospital. To find shelter for the sufferers a number of unused buildings were thrown open. I remember, especially, the St. Charles Hotel, a gloomy place, where two young girls went to look for a member of their family, reported wounded. We had tramped in vain over pavements burning with the intensity of the sun, from one scene of honor to another, until our feet and brains alike seemed about to serve us no further. The cool of those vast dreary rooms of the St. Charles was refreshing; but such a spectacle! Men in every stage of mutilation are lying on the bare boards, with perhaps a haversack or an army blanket beneath their heads,—some dying, and all suffering keenly, while waiting their turn to be attended to. To be there empty-handed and impotent nearly broke our hearts. We passed from one to the other, making such slight additions to their comfort as were possible, while looking in every upturned face in dread to find the object of our search. To supply food for the hospitals the contents of larders all over town were emptied into baskets; wine cellars long sealed and cobwebbed, belonging to the old Virginia gentry who knew good Port and Madeira, were opened by the Ituraea's spear of universal sympathy. There was not much going to bed that night, either; and I remember spending the greater part of it leaning from my window to seek the cool night air, while wondering as to the fate of those near to me. There was a summons to my mother about midnight. Two soldiers came to tell her of the wounding of one close of kin; but she was already on duty elsewhere, tireless and watchful as ever. Up to that time the younger girls had been regarded as superfluities in hospital service; but on Monday two of us found a couple of rooms where fifteen wounded men lay upon pallets around the floor, and, on offering our services to the surgeons in charge, were proud to have them accepted and to be installed as responsible nurses, under direction of an older and more experienced woman. The constant activity our work entailed was a relief from the strained excitement of life after the battle Seven Pines. When the first flurry of distress was over, the residents of those pretty houses standing back in gardens full of roses set their cooks to work, or, better still, went themselves into the kitchen, to compound delicious messes for the wounded, after the appetizing old Virginia recipes. Flitting about the streets in the direction of the hospitals were smiling, white-jacketed negroes, carrying silver trays with dishes of fine porcelain under napkins of thick white damask, containing soups, creams, jellies, thin biscuit, eggs a la crème, boiled chicken, etc., surmounted by clusters of freshly gathered flowers. A year later we had cause to pine after these culinary glories when it came to measuring out, with sinking hearts, the meager portions of milk and food we could afford to give our charges.

From our patients, when they could syllable the tale, we had accounts of the fury of the fight, which were made none the less horrible by such assistance as imagination could give to the facts. I remember they told us of shot thrown from the enemy's batteries that plowed their way through lines of flesh and blood before exploding in showers of musket-balls to do still further havoc. Before these awful missiles, it was said our men had fallen in swaths, the living closing over them to press forward in the charge.

Day by day we were called to our windows by the wailing dirge of a military band preceding a soldier's funeral. One could not number those sad pageants: the coffin crowned with cap and sword and gloves, the riderless horse following with empty boots fixed in the stirrups of an army saddle; such soldiers as could be spared from the front marching after with arms reversed and crape-enfolded banners; the passers-by standing with bare, bent heads. Funerals less honored outwardly were continually occurring. Then and thereafter the green hillsides of lovely Hollywood were frequently upturned to find resting-places for the heroic dead. So much taxed for time and for attendants were those who officiated that it was not unusual to perform the last rites for the departed at night. A solemn scene was that in the July moonlight, when, in the presence of the few who valued him most, we laid to rest one of my own nearest kinsmen, of whom in the old service of the United States, as in that of the Confederacy, it was said, "He was a spotless knight."

. . . When the tide of battle receded, what wrecked hopes it left to tell the tale of the Battle Summer! Victory was ours, but in how many homes was heard the voice of lamentation to drown the shouts of triumph! Many families, rich and poor alike, were bereaved of their dearest; and for many of the dead there was mourning by all the town. . . . [4]

Judith McGuire's Diary Continues

[June] 1st—We heard very heavy firing all day yesterday, and again to-day. At one time the roar was so continuous that I almost fancied I heard the shouts of the combatants; the firing became less about twelve o'clock, and now (night) it has ceased entirely.

7th—We have been now surrounded by the enemy for two weeks, cut off from every relative except our two households Our male relations, who are young enough, are all in the army, and we have no means off hearing one word from them The roar of the artillery we hear almost every day, but have no means of hearing the result. We see picket-fires of the enemy every night, but have, so far, been less injured by them than we anticipated. Sometimes they surround our houses, but have never yet searched them.

[June] 12th—The battled continued yesterday near the field of the day before. We gained the day! For this victory, we are most thankful. The enemy was repulsed with fearful loss; but our loss was great. The wounded were brought until a late hour last night, and today the hospitals have been crowded with ladies, offering their services to nurse, and the streets are filled with servants darting about, with waiters covered with snowy napkins, carrying refreshments of all kinds to the wounded. Many of the sick, wounded, and weary are in private houses. The roar of the cannon has ceased. Can we hope that the enemy will now retire? . . .

June 27th—Yesterday was a day of an intense excitement in the city and its surroundings. Early in the morning it was whispered about that some great movement was on foot. Large numbers of troops were seen under arms, evidently waiting for orders to march against the enemy. . . . The enemy's pickets were just across the river, and the men supposed that they were a heavy force of infantry and artillery, and the passage of the bridge would be hazardous in the extreme; yet their courage did not falter. The gallant fortieth, following by Pegram's battery, rushed across the bridge at double-quick, and with exultant shouts drove the enemy's pickets from their posts. The enemy was driven rapidly down the river to Mechanicsville, where the battle raged long and fiercely. At nine o'clock all was quiet; but not complete. The fighting is even now renewed, for I hear the firing of heavy artillery. Last night our streets were thronged until a late hour to catch the last accounts from couriers and spectators returning from the field. A bulletin from the Assistant Surgeon of the Fortieth, sent to his anxious father, assured me of the safety of some of the dearest to me; but the sickening sight of ambulances bringing in the wounded met my eye at every turn. The President, and many others, was on the surrounding hills during the fight, deeply interested spectators. The calmness of the people during the progress of the battle was marvelous. The balloons of the enemy hovering over the battle-field could be distinctly seen from the outskirts of the city, and the sound of musketry as distinctly heard. All were anxious, but none alarmed for the safety of the city. From the firing of the first gun till the close of the battle every spot favorable for observation was crowded. The tops of the Exchange, the Ballard House, the Capitol, and almost every other tall house were covered with human beings; and after nightfall the commanding hills from the President's house to the Alms-House were covered, like a vast amphitheater, with men, women and children, witnessing the grand display of fireworks—beautiful yet awful—and sending death amid those whom our hearts hold so dear. I am told (for I did not witness it) that it was a scene of unsurpassed magnificence. The brilliant light of bombs bursting in the air and passing to the ground, the innumerable lesser lights, emitted by the thousands and thousands of muskets, together with the roar of artillery and the rattling of small-arms, constituted a scene terrifically grand and imposing. What spell has bound our people? Is their trust in God, and the valor of our troops, so great that they are unmoved by these terrible demonstrations of our powerful foe? It would seem so, for when the battle was over the crowd dispersed and retired to their respective homes with seeming tranquility of persons who had been witnessing a panorama of transactions in a far-off country, in which they felt no personal interest; though they knew that their countrymen slept on their arms, only awaiting the dawn to renew the deadly conflict, on the success of which depended not only the fate of our capital, but of that splendid army, containing the material on which our happiness depends. Ah, many full, sorrowful hearts were at home, breathing out prayers for our success, or least were busy in the hospitals, administering to the wounded. Those on the hill-sides and house-tops were too nervous and anxious to stay at home—not only were they apprehensive for the city, but for the fate of those who were defending it and their feelings was too deep for expression. The same feeling, perhaps, which makes me write so much this morning. But I must go to other duties.

June 30—McClellan certainly retreating. We begin to breathe more freely; but he fights as he goes. Oh, that he may be surrounded before he gets to his gun-boats! Rumors are flying about that he is surrounded; but we do not believe it—only hope that he maybe before he reaches the river. The city is sad, because of the dead and dying, but our hearts are filled with gratitude and love. The end is not yet—oh that it were!

(ed: Information on wounded or dead relatives was difficult to obtain. Battlefield rumors prevailed and the women went from hospital to hospital, cemetery to cemetery, searching for wounded or dead relatives. They appealed to the generals and politicians for information as well, but to no avail. Hundreds of wives and mothers didn't know whether the loved ones were dead or alive. Would the battlefield dead be returned for a proper burial at home or would they be placed in a mass grave by the soldiers on either side? Not knowing was difficult at best and some women began a period of mourning assuming the worst for their loved one based upon sketchy information. Veiled faces appeared in church as a sign of grieving. Black cloth was in short supply. On a daily basis, one could hear the dirges played by military bands preceding a soldier's funeral. As a coffin would go down the street with a cap, sword and gloves on top, a rider less horse with empty boots on the stirrups completed the funeral procession. Faith was wearing thin, and women struggled to maintain the semblance of a traditional family life as they could.

4th—Our victory at Manassas complete; the fight lasted four days. General Kearney was killed in a cavalry fight at Chantilly. Beautiful Chantilly has become a glorious battlefield. The splendid trees and other lovely surroundings all gone; but it is classic ground from this time. . . .

Constance Cary Harrison's Reflections Continue

. . . My dearest mother was by now well launched in her hospital nursing at Culpeper Court House, first, among the many soldiers ill in the Methodist church, and, later, among the wounded. Her life from this time forward (afterward at Camp Winder, near Richmond) was of the hardest and most heroic kind. I have never known any woman possessed of better qualifications for her task. With a splendid physique, almost unbroken good health, a tireless hand, and a spirit of tender sympathy, she was the ideal attendant upon homesick boys from the far South, disheartened by illness at the outset of their campaign, as well as those cruelly mangled and wounded in the first fights. Almost every comfort we have nowadays in nursing was absent from the beginning, and toward the last the hospitals were unspeakably lacking. Sleeping on a soldier's bunk, rising at dawn, laboring till midnight, my mother faced death and suffering with the stout spirit that was a rock of refuge to all around her. Her record, in short, was that of a thousand other saintly women during that terrible strife. How many dying eyes looked wistfully into hers; how many anguished hands clung to hers during operations or upon death-beds! What poor lonely spirits far from home and kin took courage from her lips, to flutter feebly out into the vast unknown! What words of Christian cheer she whispered! What faith, hope, love were embodied in that tall, noble figure and sweet, sad face moving tirelessly upon her rounds! [5]

Judith Maguire's Diary Continues

Mecklenburg County, July 15—Mr.—and myself summoned here a short time ago to see our daughter, who is very ill. Found her better—she is still improving. Richmond is disenthralled—the only Yankees there are in the "Libby" and other prisons. McClellan and his "grand army" on the James near Westover are enjoying mosquitoes and bilious fevers. The weather is excessively hot. I dare say the Yankees find the "Sunny South" all that their most fervid imaginations ever depicted it, particularly on the marshes. So may it be, until the whole army melts with fervent heat. The gun-boats are rushing up and down the river, shelling the trees on the banks, afraid to approach Drewry's Bluff.

21ˢᵗ—Mr.—sick, but better to-day. This is the anniversary of the glorious battle of Manassas. Since that time, we have had many reverses, but our victories, of late, have atoned for all, except the loss of life.

28ᵗʰ— . . . A long letter from S.S., describing graphically their troubles when in Federal lines. Now they are breathing freely again. A number of servants from W. and S. H., and indeed from the whole Pamunky River, went off with their Northern friends. I am sorry for them, taken from their comfortable homes to go they know not where, and to be treated they know not how. Our Nat went, to whom I was very partial, because his mother was the maid and humble friend of my youth, and because I had brought him up. He was a comfort to us as a driver and hostler, but now that we have neither home, nor carriage, nor horses, it makes little difference to us now; but how, with his slow habits, he is to support himself, I can't imagine. The wish for freedom is natural, and if he prefers it, so far as I am concerned he is welcome to it. I shall be glad to hear that he is doing well. Mothers went off leaving children—in two instances infants. Lord have mercy upon these poor misguided creatures! I am so thankful that the scurf of the earth, of which the Federal army seems to be composed, has been driven away from Hanover. . . .

[August] 9th— . . . The Misses N. are spending the summer here. Their home in Clarke in the possession of the enemy, together with their whole property, they are dividing their time among their friends. It is sad to see ladies of their age deprived of home comforts; but like the rest of the refugees, they bear it very cheerfully. Born and reared at Westover, they are indignant in the highest degree that it should now be desecrated by McClellan's army. . . .

Lynchburg, August 20—Mr.—and myself arrived here last night, after a most fatiguing trip, by Clarksville, Buffalo Springs, then to Wolf Trap Station on the Danville road and on the Southside Railroad. The cars were filled with soldiers on furlough. . . . Lynchburg is full of hospitals, to which the ladies are very attentive; and they are said to be very well kept. I have been to a large one today, in which our old home friends, Mrs. R and Miss E.M. are matrons. Everything looks beautifully neat and comfortable. As a stranger, and having so much to do for my patient at home, I find I can do nothing for the soldiers, but knit for them all the time and give them a kind word in passing. I never see one without feeling disposed to extend my hand, and say, "God bless you."

Constance Cary Harrison's Reflections Continues

We were in Richmond when that desperate fight was fought at Antietam. . . .

By this time, in some degree keyed up to endurance of the repeated shocks of war, we went quietly about our tasks of daily life. Except for the numbers of people swathed in black met in its thoroughfares, Richmond showed little trace of its battle summer. As yet the pinch of the times did not greatly affect the home commissariat, although we refugees had to be satisfied with simple living in other people's rooms, since a whole house to ourselves could not be thought of. When asked into private houses we found tables laid, as of old, with shining silver and porcelain and snowy damask, although the bill of fare was unpretending. . . . To the very last, each refugee family shared what it had with the other; while Richmond folk threw open their broad, delightful homes to receive their friends, with or without gastronomic entertainment; lent furniture to those in need, and sent dainty little dishes to the sick. All rejoiced in each other's joys, grieved with each other's griefs. Hardships in such company were lightened of their weight. Sorrows so shared were easier to bear. [6]

Judith McGuire's Diary Continues

24th—Still no official account of the Sharpsburg fight, and no list of casualties. The Yankee loss in Generals very great—they must have fought desperately. . . .

25th—The tables were turned on Saturday, as we succeeded in driving a good many of them into the Potomac. Ten thousand Yankees crossed at Shepherdstown, but unfortunately for them, they found the glorious Stonewall there. A fight ensued at Boteler's Mill, in which General Jackson totally routed General Pleasanton and his command. The account of the Yankee slaughter is fearful. As they were re-crossing the river our cannon was suddenly turned upon them. They were fording. The river is represented as being blocked up with the dead and dying, and crimsoned with blood. Horrible to think of! But why will they have it so? At any time, they might stop fighting, and return to their own homes. We do not want their blood, but only to be separated from them as a people, eternally and everlastingly. . . .

30ᵗʰ—The *Richmond Examiner* of yesterday contains Lincoln's Proclamation, declaring all the Negroes from the 1ˢᵗ of January next! The Abolition papers are in ecstasies; as if they did not know that it can only be carried out *within their* lines, and there they have been practically free from the moment we were invaded. The *New York Tribune* is greatly incensed at the capture of Harper's Ferry; acknowledges that the battle of Sharpsburg was a disaster to them—Sumner's corps alone having lost 5,000 men in killed and wounded. It says it was the "fiercest, bloodiest, and most indecisive battle of the war." Oh, that their losses could convince them of the wickedness of this contest! But their appetite seems to grow on what it feeds upon. Blood, blood, is still their cry. My heart sickens at that thought of what our dear soldiers have yet to pass through. Arise, O God, in thy strength, and save us from our relentless foes, for they great name's sake.

Mr.—has improved so much in health that we return in a few days to Richmond, that he may again enter upon his duties of his office. Ashland is our destiny for next year; the difficulty of obtaining a house or board in Richmond has induced us to join a party of refugee friends in taking a cottage there. Our children are already there, and write that a comfortable room is awaiting us. Last night we received a message from Mrs. and Miss S., of Alexandria, that they were in this place, having run the *blockade* from their oppressed home, during the battles around Richmond, when many of the soldiers had been withdrawn, and of course the surveillance of the old town had become less severe. Mrs. D., of Alexandria and myself went directly after breakfast to see them. They had much to tell of the reign of terror through which they had gone, and nothing very satisfactory of our homes. Mrs. D.'s house was occupied as barracks and ours as a hospital. Miss—has accompanied our friend Mrs.—there one day during the last winter; it was used as a hospital, except the front rooms, which were occupied by General N. (a renegade Virginian) as headquarters. Can it be that any native of Virginia can be untrue to her now? . . . General N. married a Northern wife, which must account for his defection. The ladies drove up to our poor old home, the road winding among stumps of trees, which had been our beautiful oak grove; but one tree was left to show where it had been; they inquired for Mrs. N. She was out, and they determined to walk over the house, that they might see the state of our furniture, etc. They were up-stairs, but, on opening the door of our daughter's room, they found a lady standing at a bed, cutting out work. Mrs.—closed the door and turned to my chamber; they she found occupied by a family, children running about the room, etc.; this she afterwards found were the families of the surgeons. With no very *amicable* feelings she closed that door and went to another room, which, to her relief, was unoccupied; the old familiar furniture stood in its place, and hanging over the mantel was my husband's portrait. We left it put away with other pictures. The wardrobe, which we left packed with valuables, stood open and empty; just by it was a large travelling-trunk filled with clothing, which, she supposed, was about to be transferred to the wardrobe. She turned away, and on going downstairs met Mrs. N., who politely invited her into her (!) parlor. The piano, sofas, etc. are arranged precisely as she had been accustomed to see them arranged, she supposed by our servants, some of whom were still there. This furniture we had left carefully rolled together, and covered, in another room. . . .

W. Hanover County, October 6th—We left the University on the 4th, and finding J.B.N. on the cars, on "sick leave," I determined to stop with him here and spend a few days with my sisters, while Mr.—went to on to Richmond and Ashland. . . .

McClellan's troops were very *well-behaved* while in this neighborhood; they took nothing but what they considered contraband, such as grain, horses, cattle, sheep, etc., and induced the servants to go off. Many have gone—it is only wonderful that more did not go, considering the inducements that were offered. No houses were burned, and not much fencing. The ladies' rooms were not entered except when a house was searched, which always occurred to unoccupied houses; but I do not think that much was stolen from them. Of course, silver, jewelry, watches, etc., were not put in their way. Our man Nat, and some others who went off, have returned—the reason they assign is that the Yankees made them work too hard! It is so hard to find both families without carriage horses, and with only some mules which happened to be in Richmond when the place was surrounded. A wagon, drawn by mules, was sent to the depot for us. So many of us are together that we feel more like quiet enjoyment than we have done for months.

9th—A very pleasant day at S. H. The ladies all busily knitting for our soldiers—oh that we could make them comfortable for the winter!

10th—Bad news! The papers bring an account of the defeat of our army at Corinth (Mississippi). . . . This bringing up reinforcements, which the Yankees do in such numbers, is ruinous to us. Ah! If we could only fight them on an equal footing, we could expunge them from the face of the earth; but we have to put forth every energy to get rid of them, while they come like the frogs, the flies, the locusts, and the rest of the vermin which infested the land of Egypt, to destroy our peace.

Richmond, October 15th—Yesterday morning my sister M., J. W., and myself drove up from W. to the depot, seven miles, in a wagon, with four mules. . . .

Ashland, October 19th—We are now snugly fixed in Ashland. Our mess consists of Bishop J. and family, Major J. and wife, Lieutenant J. J. and wife (our daughter,) Mrs. S. and daughter, of Chantilly, Mrs.—, myself, and our two young daughters—a goodly number for a cottage with eight small rooms; but we are very comfortable. All from one neighborhood, all refugees, and *none able to do better*, we are determined to take everything cheerfully. Many remarks are jestingly made suggestive of unpleasant collisions among so many families in one house; but we anticipate no evils of that kind; each has her own place, and her own duties to perform; the young married ladies of the establishment are by common consent to have the housekeeping troubles; their husbands are to be masters, with the onerous duties of caterers, treasurers, etc. We old ladies have promised to give our sage advice and experience, wherever it is desired. The girls will assistant their sisters, with their nimble fingers, in cases of emergency; and the *clerical* gentlemen are to have their own way, and to do their own work without let or hindrance. All that is *required* of them is that they shall be household chaplains, and that Mrs.—shall have services every Sunday at the neglected village church. With these discreet regulations, we confidently expect a most pleasant and harmonious establishment.

Our young gentlemen are officers stationed in Richmond. Mr.—and themselves go in every morning in the cars, after an early breakfast, and return to dinner at five o'clock. J. J. and myself have free tickets to go on the cars to attend to our hospital duties. I go in twice a week for that purpose.

November 7—The snow falling rapidly—the trees and shrubs in full leaf, and rose-bushes, in bright bloom, are borne down by snow. Our poor soldiers! What are they to do to-night, without shelter, and without blankets? Everyone seems to be doing what they can to supply their wants; many persons are having carpets made into soldier's blankets . . .

November 25th—Just home from the depot. The cars have gone to Richmond, filling with non-combatants from Fredericksburg—ladies, with their children, many of whom know not where to go. They will get to Richmond after dark, and many propose staying in the cars this cold night, and seeking a resting place tomorrow. The feeling of desolation among them is dreadful. Oh how I wish that I had even one room to offer! The bombardment has not commenced, but General Lee requested last night that the women and children who had not gone should go without delay. This seems to portend hot work.

29th—Nothing of importance from the army. The people of Fredericksburg are suffering greatly from the sudden move. I know a family, accustomed to every luxury at home, now in a damp basement-room in Richmond. The mother and three young daughters cooking, washing, etc.; the father, a merchant is sick and cut off from business, friends and every thing else. Another family, consisting of mother and four daughters, in one room, are supported by the work of one of the daughters who has an office in the Note-Signing department. To keep starvation from the house is all that they can do; their supplies in Fredericksburg can't be brought to them—no transportation. I cannot mention the numbers who are similarly situated; the country is filled with them. Country houses, as usual, show a marvelous degree of elasticity. A small house accommodating any number of visitors who may apply; pallets spread on the floor; every sofa and couch *sheeted* for visitors of whom they never heard before. If the city people would do more in that way, there would be less suffering. Every cottage in this village is full; and now families are looking with wistful eyes at the ball-room belonging to the hotel, which, it seems to me, might be partitioned off to accommodate several families. The billiard-rooms are taken it is said, though not yet occupied. But how everybody is to be supported is a difficult question to decide. Luxuries have been given up long ago, by many persons. Coffee is $4 per pound, and good tea from $18 to $20; butter ranges from $1.50 to $2 per pound; lard 50 cents; corn $15 per barrel; and wheat $4.50 per bushel. We can't get a muslin dress for less than $6 to $8 per yard; calico $1.76, etc. This last is no great hardship, for we will all resort to homespun. We are knitting our own stockings; and regret that we did not learn to spin and weave. The North Carolina homespun is exceedingly pretty, and makes a genteel dress; the only difficulty is in the dye; the colors are pretty, but we have not learned the art of *setting* the wood colors; but we are improving in that art too, and when the first dye fades, we can dip them again in the dye.

30th—The Yankee army ravaging Stafford County dreadfully, but they do not cross the river. Burnside, with the "greatest army on the planet" is quietly waiting and watching our little band on the opposite side. Is he afraid to venture over? His "On to Richmond" seems slow.

13th—Our hearts are full of apprehension! A battle is going on at or near Fredericksburg. The Federal army passed over the river on their pontoons night before last. They attempted to throw their bridges over it at three places; from two of these they were driven back with much slaughter; at a third they crossed. Our army was too small to guard all points. The firing is very heavy and incessant. We hear it with terrible distinctness from our portico. God of mercy be with our people, and drive back the invaders! I ask not for their destruction; but that they may be driven to their own homes, never more to put foot on our soil; that we may enjoy the sweets of peace and security once more. Our dear boys—now as ever—I commit them into thy Hands.

14th—Firing in the direction of Fredericksburg renewed this morning, but at irregular intervals. Telegraph wires were cut. No news except from passengers in the trains. The cars are not allowed to go to the town, but stop at a point some miles before. They report every thing goes well for us, of which we were sure, from the receding sound of the cannon. Praise the Lord, O my soul, and all that is within me praise His holy name! How can we be thankful enough for such men as General Lee, General Jackson, and our glorious army, rank and file!

Nine o'clock at Night— . . . The gentlemen report many wounded on the train, but not severely. I fear it has been another bloody Sabbath. The host of wounded will pass tomorrow; we must be up early to prepare to administer to their comfort. The sound of cannon this evening was much more distant, and not constant enough for a regular fight. We are victorious again! Will they now go from our shores forever? We dread to hear of the casualties. Who may not be among the wounded tomorrow?

15th—An exciting day. Trains have been constantly passing with the wounded for Richmond hospitals. Every lady, every child, every servant in the village, has been engaged preparing and carrying food to the wounded as the car stopped at the depot—coffee, tea, soup, milk, and every thing we could obtain. With eager eyes and berating hearts we watched for those most dear to us. . . . As the cars would move off, those who were able would *shout* their blessings on the ladies of Virginia. "We will fight; we will protect the ladies of Virginia." Ah poor fellows, what can the ladies of Virginia ever do to compensate what they have done and suffered for us? . . .

Constance Cary Harrison's Reflections Continue

In December, 1862, Fredericksburg was fought. In that notable victory to Confederate arms our family met with an irreparable loss. My uncle's son, Randolph Fairfax, aged eighteen, a private in the ranks, fell beside his gun and was buried by his comrades after dark upon the spot. This youth, handsome and gifted, serious and purposeful beyond his years, the flower of his school and college, in all things worthy the traditions of his warlike ancestry, was killed by a piece of shell entering the brain, as he stood by his gun at sunset under a hot fire from the enemy's batteries. A day or two later his body, still wrapped in his soldier's blanket, was disinterred and brought through freezing weather to Richmond, where he was placed, uncoffined, on a bier before the altar in St. James's Church. An ever fresh memory is that of the sweet and noble face so unchanged, after two days' burial. Save for the cruel mark on the temple made by the piece of shell, and the golden curls matted with the clay of his rude sepulcher, he might have been asleep. He wore still the coarse flannel shirt, stained with battle smoke, in which he fell, and across him was thrown the blanket that had been his winding-sheet. When it was proposed to my uncle that the body be dressed again, he answered "No. Let my son sleep his long sleep as he fell at the post of duty." And thus, his coffin draped with the flag he had died for, Randolph Fairfax was borne to his rest in Hollywood. From camp at Fredericksburg, on December 28th, General Lee wrote to my uncle the words that follow:

"I have grieved most deeply at the death of your noble son. I have watched his conduct from the commencement of the war and have pointed with pride to the patriotism, self-denial and manliness of character he has exhibited. I had hoped that an opportunity would have occurred for the promotion he deserved; not that it would have elevated him, but have shown that his devotion to duty was appreciated by his country. Such an opportunity would undoubtedly have occurred; but he has been translated to a better world, for which his purity and piety have eminently fitted him. You do not require to be told how great his gain. It is the living for whom I sorrow. I beg you will offer to Mrs. Fairfax and your daughters, my heartfelt sympathy, for I know the depth of their grief. That God may give you and them strength to bear this great affliction, is the earnest prayer of your early friend".

"R. E. LEE."

Our stricken family, like many another, felt how nobly the great leader helped to bind up the wounds of war by words like those![7]

(ed: At the close of 1862, Southern independence seemed more distant than ever. Distraught widows and mothers focused on the basics of food, shelter and their suffering families and continued to contribute to the war effort by nursing.

With nursing, initially, women just opened up their houses to convalesce the soldiers. Women, who society had designated as weak and frivolous, were brave, strong and loving in their nursing duties. The women raised money and set up hospitals near camps and train depots without any financial support from the Medical Department of the Confederacy. In the fall of 1862, Congress finally delineated the duties of the paid and volunteer staff and set the salaries of the paid staff.

The women believed that it was God who determines who would survive a battle. Consequently, when a loved one died in a battle, many women would also have to deal with depression, guilt and a loss of faith.

Perhaps they sensed, even at this early time in the war, that their old way of life was gone forever.)

CHAPTER FOUR
1863—THE WAR CONTINUES

"How can I record the sorrow which has befallen our country?"—Judith McGuire

Judith McGuire's Diary Continues

January 8th—On the 16th of December, the day after the last entry in my diary, I went to Richmond and found B. B. at the house of Mr. P., on Grace Street, surrounded by luxury, and the recipient of unnumbered kindnesses; but so desperately ill! The surgeons had been up all night in various hospitals, and, as numerous as they were, they were sadly deficient in numbers that night. The benevolent Dr. Bolton had taken his wife and his sister, who learned the art of binding up wounds, to his hospital, and all night long they had been engaged most efficiently in their labor of love. Other ladies were engaged in services of mercy. Women who had been brought up surrounded by the delicacies and refinements of the most polished society, and who would have paled at the sight of blood under other circumstances, were bathing the most frightful gashes, while others were placing the bandages. I found B. suffering the most intense agony, and Mrs. P. agitated and anxious. No surgeon could be obtained for private houses. . . . To *cut* off his bloody clothes, replace them by fresh ones, and to administer the immense doses of morphine, was all that Mrs. P. and myself could do. At dark, Surgeons G. and B., accompanied by my brother arrived. They did what they could, but considered the case hopeless. . . .

19th— . . . Our little cottage has many pleasant visitors and I think we are as cheerful a family circle as the Confederacy can boast. We are very much occupied by our Sunday-schools—*white* in the morning and colored in the afternoon. In the week we are often busy, like the "cotter's" wife, in making "auld claes look amaist as weel as new." *"New claes"* are not attainable at present high prices; we are therefore likely to become very ingenious in fixing up "auld ones." My friend, who lately arrived from Washington, looked on very wonderingly when she saw us all ready for church. "Why, how genteel you look!" at last broke from her: "I had no idea of it. We all thought of you as suffering in every respect." I told her that the Southern women were ingenious as the men were brave; and while we cared little for dress during such anxious times, yet when our husbands and sons returned from the field we preferred that their homes should be made attractive, and that they should not be pained by the indifferent appearances of their wives, sisters, and mothers. She was still more surprised by the neatly fitting, prettily made dresses of Southern manufacture. "Are they of Virginia cloth?" she asked. No poor old Virginia has any time or opportunity for improving her manufactures, while almost her whole surface is scarred and furrowed by armies; but Georgia and North Carolina are doing much towards clothing the first ladies of the land. Sister M. has just improved my wardrobe by sending me a black alpaca dress, bought from a Potomac blockade-runner. We, ever and anon, are assisted in that way; sometimes a pound of tea, sometimes a pair of gloves, is snugged away in a friendly pocket, and, after many dangers, reaches us, and meets a hearty welcome; and what is more important still, medicine is brought in the same way, having escaped the eagle eyes of federal watchers.

February 11—For ten days past I have been at the bedside of my patient in Richmond. The physicians for the third time despaired for his life; by the goodness of God, he is again convalescent. Our wounded are suffering excessively for tonics, and I believe that many valuable lives are lost for the want of a few bottles of porter. One day a surgeon standing by B.'s bedside said to me, "He must sink in a day or two; he retains neither brandy nor milk, and his life is passing away for want of nourishment." In a state bordering on despair, I went out to houses and stores, to beg or buy porter; not a bottle was in town. At last a lady told me that a blockade-runner had brought ale, and it was at the medical purveyors. I went back to Mr. P's instantly, and told my brother (B.'s father) of the rumor. To get a surgeons' requisition and go off the purveyors was the work of a moment. In a short time he returned, with a dozen bottles of India ale. It was administered cautiously at first, and when I found that he retained it, and feebly asked for more; tears of joy and thankfulness ran down my cheeks. "Give him as much as he will take during the night." was the order of the physician. The order was obeyed, and life seemed to return to his system; in twenty-four hours he had drunk *four bottles;* he began then to take milk, and I never witnessed any thing like the reanimation of the whole man, physical and mental; The hospitals are now supplied with this life-giving beverage, and all have it who "absolutely require it" though great care is taken of it, for the supply is limited. Oh, how cruel it is that the Northern Government should have made medicines and the necessities of life to the sick and wounded contraband articles.

12th— . . . Since I have been so occupied in nursing B. I have not had as much time for the hospital, but go when I can. A few days ago, on going there in the morning, I found Miss T. deeply interested about a soldier who had been brought in the evening before. The gentlemen who accompanied him found him in the pouring rain, wandering about the streets, shivering with the cold and unable to tell his own story. The attendants quickly replaced his wet clothes by dry ones, and put him into a warm bed; rubbings and warm applications were resorted to, and a surgeon administered restoratives. Physical reaction took place, but no clearing of the mind. When soothingly asked about his name, his home and his regiment, he would look up and speak incoherently, but no light was thrown on the questions. He was watched and nursed during the night. His pulse gradually weakened, and by the break of day he was no more. That morning I found the nameless, homeless boy on the couch which I had so often seen similarly occupied. The wind had raised one corner of the sheet, and as I approached to replace it a face was revealed which riveted me to the spot. It was young, almost boyish, and, though disease and death had made sad ravages, they could not conceal delicately-carved features, a high, fair forehead, and light hair, which had been well cared for. He looked like one of gentle blood. All seemed so mysterious, my heart yearned over him, and my tears fell fast. Father, mother, sister, brothers—where are they? The morning papers represented the case, and called for information. He may have escaped in delirium from one of the hospitals! That evening, kind, gentle hands placed him in his soldier's coffin, and he had Christian burial at "Hollywood," with the lonely word "Stranger" carved upon the headboard. . . .

13th—Still in Richmond, nursing B. He was wounded this day two months ago; but such fluctuations I have never witnessed in any case. We have more hope now, because his appetite has returned. I sent over to market this morning for partridges and eggs for him, and gave 75 cents apiece for the one and $1.50 per dozen for the other. I am afraid that our currency is rapidly depreciating, and the time is approaching when, as in the old Revolution, a man had to give $300 for a breakfast . . . I have never seen more overflowing hospitality than that of this household. Many sick men are constantly refreshed from the bounties of the table. One of the elegant parlors is still in the occupancy of the wounded soldier brought here with B.; his wound was considered slight, but he suffers excessively from nervous disability, and is still unfit for service. I did feel uncomfortable that we should give Mrs. P. so much trouble, until she told me that, having no sons old enough for service, and her husband being unable to serve the country personally, except as a member of the "Ambulance Committee" they had determined that their house should be at the service of the soldiers. Last summer, during the campaigns around Richmond, they took in seven men, some of whom had to be nursed for months.

February 26th—The morning papers report firing upon Vicksburg. Several steamers have arrived lately, laden for the Confederacy. Blockade-running seems to be attended with less danger than it was, though we have lately lost a most valuable cargo by the capture of the "Princess Royal." The "Alabama" continues to perform the most miraculous feats, and the "Florida" seems disposed to rival her in brilliant exploits. . . .

28th—To-day we are all at home. It is amusing to see, as each lady walks into the parlor, where we gather around the centre-table at night, that her work-basket is filled with *clothes to be repaired.* We are a cheerful set, notwithstanding. Our winding *"reel,"* too, is generally busy. . . .

March 5th— . . . Again I have applied for an office, which seems necessary to the support of the family. If I fail, I shall try and think that it is not right for me to have it. Mr.—'s salary is not much more than is necessary to pay our share of the expenses of the mess. Several of us are engaged in making soap, and selling it, to buy things which seem essential to our wardrobes. A lady, who has been perfectly independent in her circumstances, finding it necessary to do something of the kind for her support, has been very successful in making pickles and catsups for the restaurants. Another, like Mrs. Primrose, rejoices in her success in making gooseberry wine, which sparkles like champagne, and is the best domestic wine I every drank; this is designed for the highest bidder. The exercise of this kind of industry works two ways; it supplies our wants, and gives comfort to the public. Almost every girl plaits her own hat, and that of her father, brother, and lover, if she has the bad taste to have a lover out of the army, which no girl of spirit would do unless he is incapacitated by sickness or wounds. But these hats are beautifully plaited of rye straw, and the ladies' hats are shaped so becomingly, that though a Parisian milliner might pronounce them old-fashioned, and laugh them to scorn, yet our Confederate girls look fresh and lovely in them, with their gentle countenances and bright, enthusiastic eyes; and what do we care for Parisian style, particularly as it would have to come to us through Yankee-land. The blockade has taught our people their own resources but I often think that when the great veil is removed, and reveals us to the world, we will, in some respects, be a precious set of antiques. . . . These are little things, but, proving the independence of our people, I rejoice in them. The croakers are now indulging themselves with fears of famine; they elongate their gloomy visages, and tell us, in sad accents, that butter was $3.50 per pound in market this morning, and other things in proportion. I am sorry to say it is true, and it is evident we must have scarcity; particularly of such things as butter, for the cattle must go to feed the army. The soldiers must be fed; our gardens will give us vegetables; God will give us the fruits of the earth abundantly, as in days past, and if we are reduced, which we do not anticipate, to bread and water, we will bear it cheerfully, thank God, and take courage. . . .

March 15th— . . . Richmond was greatly shocked on Friday, by the blowing up of the Laboratory, in which women, girls, and boys were employed making cartridges; ten women and girls were killed on the spot, and many more will probably die from their wounds. May God have mercy upon them. Our dear friend Mrs. S. has just heard of the burning of her house, at beautiful Chantilly. The Yankee officers had occupied it as head-quarters, and on leaving it, set fire to every house on the land, except the overseer's house and one of the servants' quarters. Such ruthless vandalism do they commit wherever they go! I expressed my surprise to Mrs. S. that she was enabled to bear it so well. She calmly replied. "God has spared my sons through so many battles, that I should be ungrateful indeed to complain of anything else." This lovely spot has been her home from her marriage, and the native place of her many children, and when I remember it as I saw it two years ago. I feel that it is too hard for her to be thus deprived of it. An officer (Federal) quartered there last winter, describing it in a letter to the New York *Herald,* says the furniture had been "removed," except a large old-fashioned sideboard. He had been indulging his curiosity by reading the many private letters which he found scattered about the house; some of which, he says, were written by General Washington, "with whom the family seems to have been connected." In this last surmise he was right, and he must have read letters from which he derived the idea, or he may have gotten it not from a letter written by George Washington did he see, for Mrs. S. was always careful of them, and brought them away with her; they are now in this house. The officer took occasion to sneer at the pride and aristocracy of Virginia, and winds up by asserting that "this establishment belongs to the mother of General J.E.B. Stuart, "to whom she is not at all related."

March 18th— . . . It seems marvelous that, in the chances and changes of war, so many of our "Seminary Hill" circle should be collected within the walls of this little cottage. Mrs. P. has once been, by permission of the military authorities, to visit her old home; she found it *used as a bakery* for the troops stationed around it. After passing through rooms which she scarcely recognized, and seeing furniture, once her own, broken and defaced, she found her way to her chamber. There was her wardrobe in its old place; she had left it packed with house-linens and other valuables, and advanced toward it, key in hand, for the purpose of removing some of its contents, when she was roughly told by a woman sitting in the room not to open that wardrobe, "There was nothing in it that belonged to her." On, how my blood would have boiled, and how I should have opened it, unless put aside by force of arms, just to have peeped in to see if my own things were still there and to take them if they were! But Mrs. P., more prudently, used a gentle remonstrance, and finding that nothing could be affected, and that rudeness would ensue, quietly left the room. We bide our time.

April 1ˢᵗ—All is quiet on the Rappahannock tonight and we are almost as still as in days gone by. The girls got up a little merriment this morning by their "April fools." The remainder of the day passed in our usual way.

April 2d—We were shocked, when the gentlemen returned, to hear of the riot which occurred in Richmond today. A mob, principally of women, appeared in the streets, attacking the stores. Their object seemed to be to get anything they could; dry-goods, shoes, brooms, meat, glassware, jewelry, were caught up by them. The military was called out—the Governor dispersed them from one part of the town, telling them unless they disappeared in five minutes, the soldiers would fire among them. This, he said, holding his watch in his hand. Mr. Munford, the President of the Young Men's Christian Association, quieted them on another street by inviting them to come to the rooms of the Association, and their wants should be supplied; many followed him—I suppose those who were really in want. Others there were, of the very worst class of women, and a great many of them who were not in want at all, which they proved by only supplying themselves with jewelry and other finery. The President was out speaking to them, and trying to secure order. The Mayor made them a speech, and seemed to influence them, but I dare say that the bayonets of the soldiers produced the most decided effect. It is the first time that such a thing has ever happened in the annals of Richmond. God grant it may be the last. I fear that the poor suffer very much; meal was selling to-day at $16 per bushel. It has been brought up by speculators. Oh that these hard-hearted creatures could be made to suffer! Strange that men, with human hearts can, in these dreadful times, thus grind the poor.

April 4ᵗʰ—Spent to-day in Richmond attending to the wounded. The mob of women came out yesterday, but in smaller numbers, and was easily put down by military authority. Today a repetition was expected, and the cannon was in place to rake the streets, but they thought discretion was the better part of valor and stayed at home. The riot, it is ascertained, was not caused by want; it was no doubt set on foot by Union influences.

(ed: As the war continued, the scarcity of food and the cost of food became an increasing problem. Calls rang out for price controls but none were instituted. There were competing demands between the military and civilians for the diminished food supply. Food production was disrupted by the skirmishes and battle. In addition the population of Richmond significantly increased with the refugees, the families of soldiers and government officials and the growth of business supporting the war effort.)

9th—On Monday I saw B. removed from the bed of suffering, on which he had been lying four months, put on a stretcher, and carried to the canal-boat, His countenance was full of joyful anticipations of home. His arm, which should have been amputated on the field, hangs lifeless by his side; and yet he expects to return to his post, that of Major of artillery, as soon as he is strong enough. Poor fellow, it is well for him to amuse himself with the idea, but he will never again be fit for any duty but that at a post. He has been a recipient of kindness from Mr. and Mrs. P. and others, which could only be experienced in this dear, warm-hearted Southern country of ours, and which he can never forget to his dying day. That night I spent with my kind friend Mrs. R., and next morning made such purchases as were absolutely necessary for our comfort. I gave for bleached cotton, which used to be sold for 12 1/2 cents, $3.50 per yard; toweling $1.25 per yard; cotton 50 cents a spool, etc. Nothing reconciled me to this extravagance but that I had sold my soap for $1 per pound!!

The enemy has retired from Vicksburg, the canal having proved a failure. Where they will reappear nobody knows. Another ineffectual attempt upon Charleston on the 7th and 8th.

Saturday night, May 9—So much has happened since I last wrote in my diary, that I can scarcely collect my thoughts to give a plain detail of facts as they occurred. Ten days ago, Mr.—and myself went in to spend two days with our children who are living in Richmond. It soon became apparent that we could not return, as the Government has taken the cars for the purpose of transporting soldiers to Fredericksburg. Hooker was among immense demonstrations, and crossing 159,000 men. They fought on Saturday, Sunday, and Monday, at different points, principally at Chancellorsville, and the enemy was repulsed at all points. . . . It is said that General Lee would have followed him, but for the dreadful storm of

Monday night and Tuesday. . . . It is pretty certain that Hooker—fighting Joe!!—had two to Lee's one and was defeated. But General Jackson was wounded severely. The great Stonewall is lost to us for a time; his left arm has been amputated, and there is a severe wounding of his right hand. Oh, I pray that God may raise him up to be a continued blessing to his country. His wife has gone to him. The best surgical skill of the army, the sympathy and anxiety of the whole South, and the prayers of the country, are his. . . .

In Richmond, the excitement was terrible. The alarm-bell pealed out its startling notes; citizens were armed, and sent out to man the batteries; extemporaneous cavalry companies were formed and sent out. Women were seen crying and wringing their hands on the streets; wild rumors were afloat; but it all ended in the raiders not attempting to get to the Richmond batteries, and the city in a few hours became perfectly quiet.

Sunday, May 10—Sad, sad tidings were brought to our cottage this morning! Washington, the youngest and darling son of our dear friend, Mrs. Stuart, has fallen. The mother and sisters are overwhelmed, while our whole house hold is shrouded in sorrow. . . .

Tuesday Evening, May 12th—How can I record the sorrow which has befallen our country! General T. J. Jackson is no more. The good, the great, the glorious Stonewall Jackson is numbered with the dead. Humanly speaking, we cannot do without him; but the same God, who raised him up, took him from us, and He, who has so miraculously prospered our cause, can lead us on without him. Perhaps we have trusted too much to an arm of flesh; for he was the nation's idol. The soldiers almost worshipped him, and it may be that God has therefore removed him. We bow in weak submission to the great Ruler of events. . . . His body was carried by yesterday in a car, to Richmond. Almost every lady in Ashland visited the car, with a wreath or a cross of the most beautiful flowers, as a tribute to the illustrious dead. An immense concourse had assembled in Richmond, as the solitary casket containing the body of a great soldier, accompanied by a suitable escort, slowly and solemnly approached the depot. The body lies in state today at the Capitol, wrapped in a Confederate flag, and literally covered with lilies of the valley and other beautiful Spring flowers.

Wednesday, 13th—I have just heard that my dear nephew, Will'by N. was wounded at Chancellorsville, and that his left leg has been amputated. He is at Mr. Marye's, near Hamilton Crossings, receiving the warm-hearted hospitality of that house, now so widely known. . . .

May 16th—We were aroused this morning before daylight, by reports that the Yankees were making a raid, and were very near this place. We all dressed hastily, and the gentlemen went out to devise a means to stop the trains which were to pass through. Though within five miles of us, they became aware that notice has been given for that purpose, and they immediately turned their steps to some more private place, where they might rob and plunder without molestation. The miserable poltroons. When on one of their raids, they will become frightened by the sudden rising of a covey of partridges, and be diverted from their course; then, they will ride bravely to a house, where they know that they will only find women and children; order meals to be prepared; search the house; take the valuables; feed their horses at the barns; take off the horses from the stables; shoot the pigs, sheep, and other stock, and leave them dead in their fields; rob the poultry-yards; then, after regaling themselves on the meals which have been prepared by force, with the threats of bayonets and pistols, they ride off, having pocketed the silver spoons and forks, which may have unwittingly been left in their way.

I have been in Richmond for two days past, nursing the wounded of our little hospital. Some of them are very severely injured, yet they are the most cheerful invalids I ever saw. It is remarked in all the hospitals that the cheerfulness of the wounded in proportion to their suffering is much greater than that of the sick. Under my care, yesterday, was one poor fellow, with a ball embedded in his neck; another with an amputated leg; one with a hole in his breast, through which a bullet had passed; another with a shattered arm; and others with slighter wounds; yet all showed indomitable spirit; evinced a readiness to be amused or interested in every thing around them; asked that the morning papers might be read to them, and gloried in their late victory; and expressed an anxiety to get well; that they may have another *"chance at them fellows."* . . .

Monday May 18th—This morning we had the gratification of a short visit from General Lee. He called and breakfasted with us, while the other passengers in the cars breakfasted at the hotel. We were very glad to see that great and good man look so well and cheerful. His beard is very long, and painfully gray, which makes him appear much older than he really is. . . .

May 20th—I feel depressed to-night. Army news from the South is bad. General Pemberton has been repulsed between Jackson and Vicksburg. . . .

25th—The enemy repulsed at Vicksburg, though it is still in a state of siege. General Johnston is there, and we hope that the best means will be used to save that heroic little city; and we pray that God may bless the means used.

27th—The news from Vicksburg by the morning's papers is very delightful and we paused for confirmation of it. The young people among the villagers and refugees have been amusing themselves, during the past two evenings, with tableaux. I am too old to do every thing in these trouble times, but one picture I regretted not seeing. It represented the Confederacy. The whole bright galaxy was there.—South Carolina in scarlet, resistant Virginia, grave and dignified, yet bright with hope, seemed to be beckoning Kentucky that stood beyond the threshold, her eyes cast down with shame and suffering; Maryland on the threshold, but held back by a strong hand; all the rest of the fair sisters were there in their appropriate places, forming a beautiful picture.

(ed: To raise funds for charities, upper-class women organized plays or tableaux. Young women were in costume and represented seceding states, confederate symbols, etc. Ornate stages and patriotic songs added to the event. However, these were not without controversy. Women in the middle or lower classes felt that such entertainment in a time of austerity and war was inappropriate.)

May 28—Hospital day—The wounded cheerful and doing well. I read, distributed books, and talked with them. They are always ready to be amused, or to be instructed. I have never but in one instance had an unpleasant word or look from any which I endeavored to treat with kindness in any way. Bible reading is always kindly received. . . .

16th—The morning papers gave a telegram from General Lee announcing that General Early's brigade had taken Winchester by storm. So again Winchester and all that beautiful country, Clark, etc. are disenthralled.

It is said that our army will go to Pennsylvania. Thus I dread; but it is in God's hands, I believe, for good and not for evil.

21st—We hear of fights and rumor of fights. It is said the Ewell's Division captured 6,000 prisoners at Winchester, and that General Edward Johnson went to Berryville and captured 2,000 that were on their way to reinforce Millroy. They have driven the enemy out of the Valley, so that now we have possession of it once more. Our cavalry has been as far as Chambersburg, Pennsylvania, but I do not know what they accomplished.

Saturday Evening—Just heard from W. and S. H.; both terribly robbed by the raiders in the last three days. All of my brother's horses and mules were taken. Some of the servants were forced off, who staid faithfully by them, and resisted all the Yankee entreaties twice before. Many attempted to burn the wheat, which is shocked in the field, but an opportune rain made it too wet to burn. The raiders came up the river, destroying crops, carriages, etc., stealing horses and cattle, and carrying off the servants from every plantation. . . .

Wednesday—Many exciting rumors to-day about the Yankees being at Hanover Court-House, within a few miles of us. They can be traced everywhere by the devastation which marks their track. There are also rumors that our army is in Pennsylvania. So it may be! We are harassed to death with their ruinous raids, and why should not the North feel it in its homes? Nothing but their personal suffering will shorten the war. I don't want women and children to suffer; nor should they follow their example, and break through and steal. I want our warfare carried out in a more honorable way, but I do want our men and horses to be fed on the goods on Pennsylvania. I want the fine dairies, pantries, granaries, meadows and orchards of the rich farmers of Pennsylvania to be laid open to our army; and I want it all paid with *Confederate money, which will be good at some future day.* I want their horses, our cavalry and wagons, in return for the hundreds of thousands that they have taken and I want their fat cattle driven in Virginia to feed our army. . . .

July 3rd— . . . Our troops seem to be walking over Pennsylvania without let or hindrance. They have taken possession of Chambersburg, Carlisle, and other smaller towns. They surrendered without firing a gun. I am glad to see that General Lee orders his soldiers to respect private property; but it will be difficult to make an incensed soldiery, whose houses have in many instances been burned, crops wantonly destroyed, horses stolen, negroes persuaded off, hogs and sheep shot down and left in the field in warm weather—it will be difficult to make such sufferers remember the Christian precept of returning good for evil. The soldiers in the hospital seem to think that many a private torch will be applied "just for revenge." It was in vain that I quoted them, "Vengeance is mine; I will repay, saith the Lord." One stoutly maintained that he would like to go north "just to burn two good houses; one in return for my own house on [the] Mississippi River; the other for that of my brother-in-law, both of which they burned just after landing from their boat, with no pretense at an excuse for it; and when I think of my wife and children homeless, I feel as if I could set all Yankeedom in a blaze." Poor fellow! He became so excited that he arose in his bed, as if impatient to be off and at his work of vengeance. . . .

Monday morning— . . . About one o'clock I was awakened by E. leaning over me, and saying in a low, tremulous tone, "Mother, get up, the Yankees are coming." We sprang up, and they were at the telegraph office, immediately opposite. In an instant the door was broken down with a crash and the battery and other things thrown out. Axes were at work cutting down the telegraph-poles, while busy hands were tearing up the railroad. A sentinel sat on his horse at our gate as motionless as if both men and horse had been cut from a block of Yankee granite. We expected every moment that they would come to the house, or at least go to the hotel opposite us; but off they went to the spot. There was dead silence, except an occasional order, "Be quick," Keep a sharp look-out," etc., etc. The night was moon light, but we dressed ourselves and sat in the dark; we were afraid to open the window-shutters or to light a lamp, lest they might be attracted to the house. We remained this way perhaps two hours, when the flames suddenly burst from the depot. All parts of the building seemed to be burning at once; also immense piles of wood and of plank. The conflagration was brilliant. As soon as the whole was fairly blazing the pickets were called in, and the whole party dashed off with demonic yells. Soon after, as the dawn began to break upon us, doors were thrown open, and the villagers began to sally forth to the fire. In a short time all of us were there, from every house—even the babies; and as it became daylight, an amusing group was revealed. Every one dressed in the dark, and all manner of costumes were to be seen—dressing—gowns, cravat less old gentlemen, young ladies in curl-papers, collars pinned awry, etc. Some ladies presented themselves in full costume—handsome dresses, lace collars, ear-rings and breastpins, watches, etc.-giving as a reason, that, if they were burnt out, they would at least save their best clothes—forgetting that a Yankee soldier has an irresistible *penchant* for watches and other jewelry. Some of us were more cautious, and had put all our valuables in *unapproachable* pockets—the pockets to a lady's dress not having proved on all occasions a place of safety. The loss to the railroad company will be considerable; to the public very small, for they are already replacing the broken rail, and the telegraph was put in operation yesterday.

The morning papers give the Northern account of a battle in Gettysburg, Pennsylvania. It gives the victory to the Federals, though it admits a very heavy loss on their side. . . . We pause for the truth.

8th—Accounts from Gettysburg are very confused. Nothing seems to be known certainly; but Vicksburg has fallen! So say the rumor: and we are afraid not to believe. It is a terrible loss to us; but God has been so good to us heretofore that we can only say, "It is the Lord." . . . Many troops have passed here to-day, for what point we know not. Our anxiety is very great. Our home is blessed with health and comfort.

July 11—Vicksburg was surrendered on the 4th of July. The terms of capitulation seems marvelously generous for such a foe. What can the meaning be? General Lee had a most bloody battle near Gettysburg. Our loss was fearful. . . .

July 12—The enemy is again before Charleston. Lord, have mercy on the efforts of our people!

(ed: The civilians began to feel the hopelessness of their cause. Their prayers to God had been seemingly unanswered. Everything had changed and they now face additional losses of their "flower of youth. The long lists of dead and wounded appeared in the daily newspapers. Conflicting information dashes

hopes into despair. They also were buffeted with shortages and inflation. Their faith was giving away to doubt and loss of hope.)

14th—To-day spent in the hospital; a number of the wounded from the fatal field of Gettysburg They are not severe wounded, or they could not have been brought so far. . . .

Alas! Alas! The South now weeps for some of her bravest sons. But, trying as it is to record the death of those dear boys, it is harder still to speak of those of our own house and blood. Lieutenant B. H. McGuire, our nephew, the bright, fair-haired boy, from whom we parted last summer at Lynchburg as he went on his way to the field, full of buoyancy and hope is among the dead at Gettysburg. Also, Austin Brockenbrough of Essex County. Virginia has no son to whom a brighter future opened. His talents, his education, his social qualifications, his affectionate symphony with all around him, are all laid low. Oh, may God be with those of whose life they seemed a part! It is hard to think of so many of our warm-hearted, whole-souled, brave, ardent Southern youths, now sleeping beneath the cold clods of Pennsylvania. We can only hope that they day is not too far distant when we may bring their dear bodies back to their native soil.

July 15th—In Richmond to-day, I saw my old friend, Mrs. E.R.C., looking after her sons. One was reported "wounded;" the other "missing." This sad word may mean that he is a prisoner; it may mean worse. She can get no clue to him. His company has not come, and she is very miserable. Two mothers, one from Georgia, another from Florida, have come in pursuit if their sons, and are searching the hospitals for them. They were not in our hospital, and we could give them no information. There is much unhappiness abroad among our people that than I have ever seen before. Sometimes I wish I could sleep until it was over—a selfish wish enough; but it is hard to witness so much sorrow which you cannot alleviate.

July 18—This day two years ago the battle of Bull Run was fought, a kind of prelude to that of Manassas, on the 21st. Since that time what scenes have been enacted! Battles have been fought by scores, and lives, precious lives, have been sacrificed by thousands, and that, too, of the very flower of our country. . . . The news of the New York riots, which they got up in opposition to the draft, is cheering! Oh! That they could not get up another army, and would fight each other!

July 23—Spent the day at the hospital. Mr.—has just received a post chaplaincy from the Government, and is assigned to the Officers' Hospital on Tenth Street. For this we are very thankful, as the performance of the duties of the ministerial office is in all respects congenial to his taste and feeling. I pray that God may give him health and strength for the office!

28th—The girls are in Richmond, staying at Dr. G's. They went to attend a tournament to be given to-day by General Jenkins's Brigade, stationed near Richmond; but this morning the brigade was ordered to go south, and great was the disappointment of the young people. They cannot feel as we do during these gloomy times, but are always ready to catch the "passing pleasure as it flies," forgetting that, in the best times,

> "Pleasures are like poppies spread;
> You seize the flower, the bloom is shed."

And how much more uncertain are they now, when we literally cannot tell what a day may bring forth, and none of us know, when we arise in the morning, that we may not hear before noonday that we have been shorn of all that makes life dear!

July 29—A letter of farewell from the Valley, written as the enemy's lines were closing around our loved ones there. It is painful to think of their situation, but they are in God's hands. . . . The fearful list of killed and wounded, when so many of our nearest and dearest are engaged, is too full of anguish to anticipate without as sinking of heart which I have never known before. . . . I was in Richmond this morning and bought a calico dress, for which I gave $2.50 per yard, and considered it a bargain; the new importations have run up to $3.50; and $4 per yard. To what are we coming?

August 10—Spent this morning in the house of mourning. Our neighbor Mrs. S. has lost her eldest son. The disease was "that most fatal of Pandora's train," consumption. He contracted it in the Western Army. His poor mother watched the ebbing of his life for several months, and last night he died most suddenly. That young soldier related to me an anecdote, some weeks ago, with his short, oppressed breathing and broken sentences, which showed the horrors of this fratricidal war. He said the day after the battle in Missouri, in the fall of 1861, he, among others, was detailed to bury the dead. Some Yankee soldiers were on the field doing the same thing. As they turned over a dead man, he saw a Yankee stop, look intently, and then run to the spot with an exclamation of horror. In a moment he was on his knees by the body, in a paroxysm of grief. It was his brother. They were Missourians. The brother now dead had emigrated south some years before. He said that before the war communication had been kept up between them, and he had strongly suspected that he was in the army; he had consequently been in constant search of his brother. The Northern and Southern soldiers then united in burying him, who was his brother in arms of the one, and the mother's son of the other!

September 8— . . . The year of sojourn at this cottage is nearly over. Our mess must be broken up, as some of our gentlemen are ordered away. We have had a very pleasant time, and it is painful to dissolve our social relations. Not one of our families is provided with a home; we are all looking out for lodging and find it very difficult to get them. The change of home, habits, and association is very trying to old persons; the variety seems rather pleasant to the young.

September 16—This home is to be sold on the 29th, so we must all find resting-places before the time. But where? Room-rent in Richmond is enormously high. We may get one very small cottage here for forty dollars per month, but it has the reputation of being unhealthy. Our connection, Mr. P., is looking out for a home, and we may get one together. It would be delightful to have him and the dear girls with us. No one thinks of boarding; almost all the boarding-house keepers rent out their rooms and refugees keep house in them as cheaply as they choose,

Richmond 24th—We have all been scattered. The Bishop has obtained good rooms; the other members of the household are temporally fixed. We are here with our son, looking for rooms every day; very few are vacant. And they are too high for our means. We shall probably have to take the little cottage at Ashland, notwithstanding its reputation-either the cottage or country-house near Richmond, about which we are in correspondence with a gentleman. The plan will be carried out, and work well if the Lord pleases, and with this assurance, we should be satisfied; but still we are restless and anxious. Our ladies, who have been brought up in the greatest luxury, are working with their hands to assist families. The offices given to ladies have been filled long ago, and yet I hear of a number of applicants. Mr. [Secretary of the Treasury Christopher G.] says that one vacancy will bring a hundred applications. Some ladies plait straw hats for sale; I saw one sold this morning for twenty dollars—and their fingers, which have not been accustomed to work for their living, plait on merrily; they can dispose of them easily; and so far from being ashamed of it, they take pride in their own handiwork. I went to see Mrs.—today, the daughter of one of our gentlemen high in position, and whose husband was a wealthy landowner in Maryland. I found her sitting at her sewing machine, making an elaborate shirt-bosom. She said she took in sewing and spoke of it very cheerfully. "How can we rent rooms and live on captains' pay?" She began by sewing for brothers and cousins, then for the neighbors, and now for anybody who will give it to her she laughingly added that she thought she would hang out her sign, "plain sewing done here." We certainly are a *great people,* women as well as men. This lady, and all other ladies, has always places at their frugal tables for hungry soldiers. Many ladies take in copying.

(ed: The war opened up opportunities for women in business. Factory work, teaching in schools, and running small businesses became respectable work for them. Government work, like signing Confederate bills, sewing uniforms and knapsacks, became available to women with political connections. These pay in these government positions, however, could not keep up with the hyper-inflation that was being experienced.)

25th—There has been a great battle in the West, at Chickamauga, in Tennessee, between Bragg and Rosecrans. We are gloriously victorious!

28th— . . . I am still anxious about our home. Mr.—is sick, and the prospect of getting a house diminishing. Perhaps I should take comfort from the fact that a great many persons are homeless as well as ourselves. If Mr.—were well, I should not feel so hopeless. The girls, too, are visiting the country, expecting us to get an *impossible* home, and I do dislike to disappoint them. Oh, that we could be perfectly satisfied, knowing that we are in the Lord's hands!

Cedar Hill October 4—We came to Ashland on the 29th, to attend the sale of the house in which we lived the past year. We got a few pieces of furniture, and determined to rent the little cottage. We spent the night at Mrs. T—'s and came here next morning, and now collecting mops, brooms and the various *et ceteras* necessary for housekeeping. As refugee friend, who will change her location, she has lent us her furniture so that we expect to be very snug. Of course, we shall have no curtains nor carpets, which are privation in our old age, but the deficiencies, must be made up by large wood fires and bright faces. The war has taught us useful lessons, and we can make ourselves comfortable and happy on much less than we ever dreamed of before.

October 24—Since writing in my dairy, our plans have been entirely changed. Our old friend, Mrs. R., offered us rooms in Richmond, on such terms as are within our means, and a remarkable circumstance connected with it. It is that they are in the house which my father once occupied, and the pleasant chamber which I now occupy I left this month twenty-nine years ago. It is much more convenient to live in Richmond than in Ashland, so that we have rented the little cottage to another. One room answers the purpose of dining-room and sleeping-room, by putting a large screen around the bed; the girls have a room, and we used the parlor of the family for entertaining our guests. For this we pay $60 per month and half the gas bills.

But this has been a sad month to me, and I find it very difficult to bring my mind to the ordinary affairs of life. On the 11th of this month, our nephew, Captain William B Newton, was killed while leading a Calvary charge in Culpeper County. We have the consolation of believing that this redeemed spirit has passed into heaven; but to how many has the earth been left desolate! His young wife and three lovingly children; his father, mother, sisters, brothers, uncles and aunts, have seen the pride of their hearts pass away. His country mourns him as a great public loss. The bar, the legislative hall, and the camp looked to him as one to whom their best interests would hereinafter be entrusted; in war, as one of the most gallant officers on the field. . . . I long and yet dread to go to that once bright home, the light of which has faded forever.

I was shocked to hear that on the fatal Sunday on which my darling William fell, three of the E[piscopal] H[igh] S[chool] boys had come to a glorious, though untimely end, on the same field. . . . These dear boys! Oh, I trust that they sprang from the din of the battle-field to the peace of heaven! Lord, how long must we suffer such things?

27th— . . . It is strange how we go from month to month, living in the present, without any prospect for the future. We had some sweet, sad talk of our dear William. She says he was prepared, and God took him. At his funeral, his pastor took out his last letter from him, but became so overwhelmed with tears that he could not read it. It is right, and we must submit; but it is a bitter trial to give up one we loved so dearly.

28th—Our niece, M. P., came for me to go with her on a shopping trip expeditions. It makes me sad to find our money depreciating so much, except that I know it was worse during the old Revolution A merino dress cost $12.50, long cloth $5.50 per yard, fine cotton stockings $6 per pair; handkerchiefs, for which we gave fifty cents before the war, are now $5. There seems to be no scarcity of dry-goods of the ordinary kinds; bombazines, silks, etc., are scarce and very high; carpets are not to be found—they are too large to run the blockade from Baltimore, from which city many of our goods come.

November 9—We are now quite comfortably fixed, in a way what was once my mother's chamber, and most unrepentantly we have a carpet. The other day, while entertaining some friends, in this chamber by night, dining-room by day, and parlor even and anon, Mrs. Secretary Mallory walked in, who, like ourselves, has had many ups-and-downs during the Confederacy, and therefore her kind heart knows exactly how to sympathize with others. While talking away, she suddenly observed that there was no carpet on the floor, and exclaimed, "Mrs. McGuire, you have no carpet! My boxes have just come from Montgomery, where I left them two years ago, filled with carpets and bedding. I have five, and I will lend you one. Don't say a word; I couldn't be comfortable and think of you with this bare floor. Mr.—is too delicate for it, and you are both too old to begin now on an uncarpeted room." An hour after she left us a servant came with the carpet, which was soon tacked down, and gives a home-like, comfortable air to the room.

11th—Just received a visit from my nephew, W[illoughby] N[ewton], who is on his way to Fauquier [County] to be married. I had not seen him since he lost his leg. He is still on crutches, and it makes my heart bleed to see him walk with such difficulty. I believe, neither war, pestilence, nor famine could put an end to the marrying and giving in marriage which is constantly going on . . .

13th—My appointment to a clerkship in the Commissary Department has been received, with a salary of $125 per month. The rooms are not ready for us to begin our duties, and Colonel R—has just called to tell me one of the requirements. As our duties are those of accountants, we are to go through a formal examination in arithmetic. If we do not, as the University boys say "pass", we are considered incompetent, and of course are dropped from the list of appointees. This requirement may be right, but it is certainly seems to me both provoking and absurd that I must be examined in arithmetic by a commissary major young enough to be my son. If I could afford it, I would give up the appointment, but, as it is, must submit with the best grace possible, particularly as other ladies my age have to submit to it.

December 4—On Friday last there was a severe fight on the Rapidan, at Germanna Ford. The enemy was splendidly repulsed.

December 12—Today I was examined on arithmetic—"Denominate numbers, vulgar and decimal fraction, tare and tret," etc., etc. by Major Brewer of the Commissary department. I felt as if I had returned to my childhood. But for the ridiculousness of the thing, I dare say I should have been embarrassed. On Monday I am to enter on the duties of the office. We are to work from nine to three.

We have just received from our relatives in the country some fine Irish and sweet potatoes, cabbages, butter, sausages, chives and a ham; and from a friend in town two pounds of very good green tea. These things are very acceptable, as potatoes are twelve dollars per bushel, pork and bacon two dollars fifty cents per pound, and good tea at twenty-five dollars per pound. How are the poor to live? Though, it is said that the *poor genteel* are the real sufferers. Money is laid aside for paupers by everyone who can possibly do it, but persons who do not let their wants be known are the really poor.

Sunday Dec. 13—The first anniversary of the battle of Fredericksburg, where we lost so many valuable lives, and where the Federals were thoroughly whipped. Since that time we have lost so many lives, which nothing can repay; but we hold our own, have some victories, and have been the whole much blessed by God. . . .

CHAPTER FIVE
1864—THE WAR CONTINUES

"Thus, we bury, one by one, the dearest, the brightest, the best of our domestic circles."—Judith McGuire

Judith McGuire's Diary Continues

January 1, 1864— . . . Thus we bury, one by one, the dearest, the brightest, the best of our domestic circles. Now, in our excitement, while we are scattered, and many of us our homeless, these separations are poignant, nay, overwhelming; but how can we estimate that sadness of heart which will pervade the South when the war is over, and we are again gathered together around the family hearths and altars, and find the circles broken? One and another gone. Sometimes the father and husband, the beloved head of the household, in whom centered all that life made dear. Again the eldest son and brother of the widowed home, to whom all looked for guidance and direction; or, perhaps, that bright youth, on whom we have not ceased to look still as a child, whose fair, beardless check we had but now been in the habit of smoothing with our hands in fondness—one to whom mother and sisters would always give the good-night kiss, as his peculiar due, and repress the sigh that would arise at the thought that college or business days had almost come to take him from us. Another we will remember the mixed feeling of hope and pride when we first saw the household pet don his jacket of gray and shoulder his musket for the field; how we would be bright and cheerful before him, and turn to our chambers to weep oceans of tears when he is fairly gone. And does he, too, sleep his last sleep? Does our precious one fill a hero's grave? O God! Help us, for the wail is in the whole land! "Rachael is weeping for her children, and will not be comforted, because they are not." In all the broad South there will be scarcely a fold without its missing lamb, a fireside without its vacant chair. And yet we must go on. It is our duty to rid our land of invaders; we must destroy the snake which is devouring to entwine us in its coils, though it drains our hearts blood. . . .

January 3—Entered the duties of my office on the 30ᵗʰ of December. . . . The ladies, thirty-five in number, are of all ages, and representing various parts of Virginia, also Maryland and Louisiana. Many of them are refugees. It is melancholy to see how many wear mourning for brothers or other relatives, the victims of war. One sad young girl sits near me, whose two brothers have fallen on the field, but she is too poor to buy mourning. I found many acquaintances, and when I learned the history of others, it was often of fallen fortunes and destroyed homes. . . . I am now obligated to visit the hospital in the afternoon and I give it two evenings in the week. It is a cross to me not to be able to give more time; but we have very few patients just now, so it makes very little difference.

January 15—My occupation at home just now is as new as that in the office—it is shoe-making. I am busy upon the second pair of gaiter boots. They are made of canvas, presented to me by a friend. . . . The gaiters are cut out by a shoemaker, stitched and bound by the ladies, then sold by a shoemaker, for a moderate sum of fifty dollars. . . . The girls make beautifully fitting gloves of dark flannel, cloth, linen, and any other material we can command. . . .

February 15 . . . Prices of provisions have risen enormously—bacon $8 per pound, butter—$15, etc. . . . The clerks' salaries, too, have been raised to $250 per month, which sounds very large; but when you remember that flour is $300 per barrel, it sinks into insignificance.

28ᵗʰ—Our hearts ache for the poor. A few days ago, as E. was walking out, she met a wretchedly dressed woman, of miserable appearance, who said she was seeking the Young Men's Christian Association, where she hoped to get assistance and work to do. E. carried her to the door, but it was closed, and the poor woman's' wants were pressing. She then brought her home, supplied her with food, and told her to return to see me the following afternoon. She came, with an honest countenance and manner and told me her story. Her name is Brown; her husband had been a workman in Fredericksburg; he joined the army, and was killed at the second battle of Manassas. Many of her acquaintances in Fredericksburg fled last winter during the bombardment; she became alarmed, and with her three children fled too. She tried to get work in Richmond; sometimes she succeeded, but could not supply her wants. A kind woman lent her a room and a part of a garden, but it was outside of the corporation; although it saved house-rent, it debarred her from the relief of the associations formed for supplying the city poor with meal, wood, etc. She evidently had been a situation little short of starvation. I asked her if she could get bread enough for her children by her work. She said she could sometimes, and when she could not, she "got turnip-tops from a piece in her garden, which were now putting up smartly, and she boiled them, with a little salt, and fed them on that". "But do they satisfy your hunger," said I? "Well, it is something to go upon for a while, but it does not stick by us like bread does, and then we gets hungry again, and I am afraid to let the children eat them too often, lest they should get sick; so I tries to get them to go to sleep; and sometimes the woman in the next room will bring the children her leavings, but she is monstrous poor." When I gave her meat for her children, taken from the bounty of our Essex friends, tears of gratitude ran down her cheeks; she said they "had not seen meat for so long." Poor thing, I promised her that her case should be known, and that he should not suffer so again.

A soldier's widow shall not suffer from hunger in Richmond. It must not be, and will not be when her case is known. Others are now interested for her. This evening Mrs. R. and myself went in pursuit of her; but though we went through all the streets and lanes of "Butcher Flat" and other vicinities, we could get no clue to her. We went into many small and squalid-looking houses, yet we saw no such abject poverty as Mrs. Brown's. All who needed it were supplied with meat by the corporation, and many were supporting themselves with Government work. One woman stood at a table cutting out work; we asked her the stereotyped question—"Is there a very poor widow named Brown in this direction?" "No, ladies; I knows two Mrs. Browns, but they ain't so poor, and ain't no widows nuther." As neither of them were our Mrs. B., we turned away, but she suddenly exclaimed, "Ladies, will one of you read my husband's last letter to me? For you can see I can't read writing." As Mrs. R. took it, she remarked that it was four weeks old, and asked it if no one had read it to her? "Oh yes, a gentleman has read it to me four or five times, but you see I loves to hear it, for maybe I shan't hear from him no more." The tears now poured down her cheeks. "He always writes to me every chance, and it has been so long since he wrote that, and they tell me that they have been fighting, and maybe something has happened to *him.*" We assured her that there had been no fighting—not even a skirmish. This quieted her, and Mrs. R. read the badly written but affectionate letter, in which he expresses his anxiety to see her and her children, and his inability to get a furlough.

She then turned to the mantelpiece, and with evident pride took from a nail an old felt hat, through the crown of which was two bullet-holes. It was her husband's hat, through which a bullet had passed in the battle of Chancellorsville, and, as she remarked, must have come "very nigh grazing his head." We remarked upon it being a proof of his bravery, which gratified her very much; she then hung it up carefully, saying that it was just opposite her bed, and she never let it be out of her sight. She said we wanted her husband to fight for his country, and not to stand back, like some women's husbands, to be drafted; she would have been ashamed of that, but she felt uneasy, because something told her that he would never come back. Poor woman! We felt very much interested in her, and tried to comfort her.

March 10—There has been much excitement in Richmond about Kilpatrick's and Dahlgren's raids and the death of the latter. The cannon roared around the city, the alarm-bell rang, the reserves went out; but Richmond was safe, and we felt no alarm. As usual they did all the injury they could to country-people, by pillaging and burning. They steal everything they can; but the people have become very adroit in hiding. Bacon, flour, etc., are put into the most mysterious places; plate and handsome china are kept underground; horses are driven into dense words, and the cattle and sheep are driven off. It astonishes, though much is taken, how much is left. I suppose the raiders are too much hurried for close inspection.

April 1—My diary has been somewhat neglected, for after looking over commissary accounts for six hours in the day, and attending to home or hospital duties in the afternoon, I am too much wearied to write much at night. There are reports of movements in the armies which portend bloody work as the season advances.

We continue quite comfortable at home. Of course, provisions are scarce; but thanks to our country friends and relatives, we have never been obligated to give up meat entirely. . . . Groceries are extremely high. We are fortunate in buying ten pounds of tea, when it only sold for $22 per pound. White sugar is not to be thought of by a person of moderate means. Milk is very scarce and high, so that we have only had it once for many months. . . .

On going down-stairs this evening, I found my friend Mrs. Upshur awaiting me in the parlor. She is the widow of the Hon. Abel P. Upshur, Secretary of War in Mr. Tyler's administration, whose untimely end we remember so well. She is a refugee from Washington, and called to ask me to assist her in finding a room to accommodate herself, her sister, and her little grandson. Her present room, in the third story of a very nice house, suited her very well, but the price was raised every month, until it had become beyond her means. She is rich, but it is almost impossible for her to get funds from Washington. To obtain a room is a most difficult task, but I cheerfully promised her to do what I could; but that I first must go up the street to get some flour, for as it was $300 per barrel; we could not get one, but must purchase it at $1.25 per pound, until we could get some wheat, which we were expecting from the country, and have it ground. She at once insisted on lending me flour until ours was ground; this being agreed to, we continued on our walk in pursuit of a room. We naturally talked of the past. She related to me a circumstance which occurred when I was a young girl, and was a striking illustration of the change which time and the war had brought on us both. She said that during the political Convention of 1829-30, she came to Richmond with her husband, who was a member of it. The first entertainment to which she was invited was given at my father's house. When she entered the room my mother was standing about the centre of it, receiving her guests, and seeing that Mrs. Upshur was young and a perfect stranger, she took her by the hand and seated her by Mrs. Madison, at the same time introducing her to that celebrated woman. She said that it was one of the most pleasant evenings of her life, and she looked back on it, with peculiar satisfaction, for she was introduced to Mr. Madison, Mr. Monroe, Mr. Benjamin Watkins Leigh, and many others of the celebrated men of the day, who were attending the Convention. Could we then have looked through the vista of time, and seen ourselves in this same city, the one looking for a cheap room in somebody's third story, the other looking for *cheap bread* would we have believed it? The anecdote saddened us both for a time, but we soon recovered and went on our way in cheerful, hopeful conversation. But we did not find the room.

April 25— . . . This city is quite excited by Mr. Memminger having ordered off the Note-signing department, consisting entirely of ladies, to Columbia, South Carolina. It has caused much distress, for many of them whose living depends upon the salary, can't possibly go. Mothers can't leave their children, nor wives their husbands No one seems to understand the motive which promoted the order. It seems to be very arbitrary. It is thought by some persons that all the departments will be ordered off. I trust not; for among many others, would be obligated to resign and I can't imagine we would live without the salary. . . .

The enemy threatens Richmond, and is coming against it with an immense army. They boast that they can and will have it by this summer; but, with the help of God, we hope to drive them back gain. Our government is making every effort to defeat them. I don't think that anyone doubts our ability to do it; the awful loss of life necessary upon the fights is what we dread.

May 2— . . . The Bishop says it is too expensive here for his income, and so it is for everybody's income, but were we to leave it we should have none; our whole dependence is now upon the Government, except the interest on a small amount invested in Confederate bonds.

Tuesday Morning, May 3 . . . On Saturday our President had a most heart-rending accident in his family. His little son was playing on the back-portico, fell over, and was picked up apparently lifeless. Both parents were absent, nor did they get home in time to see their child alive. The neighbors collected around him, physicians were immediately called in, but the little fellow could not be roused; he breathed for about three-quarters of an hour. His devoted parents returned to find their boy, whom they left two hours before full of "life in every limb," now cold in death. They have the deep sympathy of the community.

May 6—The Federals are this morning ascending James River, with a fleet of thirty-nine vessels—four monitors among them. The battle between Lee and Grant is imminent. God help us! We feel strengthened by the prayers of so many good people. All the city seems quiet and trusting. . . . Grant's force is said to be between one hundred and fifty and one hundred and eighty thousand men. The "battle is not always to the strong." As we have often experienced during the past three years.

Constance Cary Harrison's Reflections

"No feeling heart in Richmond failed to yield tender sympathy to the President's family in the calamity that befell them when little, merry, happy "Joe," petted by all visitors to the Executive Mansion—he who, when his father was in the act of receiving official visitors, once pushed his way into the study and, clad only in an abbreviated night-gown, insisted upon saying his evening prayer at the President's knee—fell from the porch in the rear of their dwelling and was picked up dead on the brick pavement underneath. From Burton Harrison, upon whom devolved all arrangements in behalf of the stricken parents, we heard a pitiful tale of the mother's passionate grief and the terrible self-control of the President, who, shutting himself in his own room, had walked the floor without ceasing all of the first night. To the bier of the little lad, it seemed that every child in Richmond brought flowers and green leaves.

The battle of the Wilderness, on May 6, 1864, and its terrible sequel, of musketry setting fire to brush and undergrowth on the field where dead and wounded were alike wrapped in flame and smoke during one long appalling night; the serious wounding of Lieutenant-General Longstreet; the battles of Spotsylvania Court House on May 10 and 12, with the death of Stuart near the Yellow Tavern on the later date, renewed all the old strain of continual yearning over the fortunes of our army. The horrors of the slaughter at Cold Harbor, on June 3, in which the Union army lost over 13,000 men, the result, it was said, of little over one hour's fighting, and the beginning of the siege of Petersburg, focused emotion. It did not seem we could stand more of these bludgeonings of Fate.

My mother, for some time inactive in her nursing, declared she could rest no longer. She had been out to visit the hospital at Camp Winder, in a barren suburb of the town, where the need of nurses was crying. My aunt, Mrs. Hyde, deciding to accompany her, they were soon installed there, my mother as division matron, in charge of a number of rude sheds serving as shelter for the patients, my aunt controlling a dispensary of food for the sufferers. It had been proposed that I should remain in town with friends, but my first glance at my mother's accommodations in the camp made me resolve to share them and try to do my part. To the nurses and matrons was allotted one end of a huge Noah's Ark, built of unpainted pine, divided by a partition, the surgeons occupying the other end. Near by were the diet kitchens and store-rooms, around which were gathered wards and tents, the whole camp occupying an arid, shade-less, sun-baked plain, without grass or water anywhere, encircled by a noxious trench too often used to receive the nameless debris of the wards. To my mother, and myself as a volunteer aid to her, was assigned a large bare room with rough-boarded walls and one window, a cot in each corner, two chairs, a table, and washing apparatus. Then a kind lady coming to see us and declaring she was about to remove to the country and had nowhere to store a roomful of furniture, we fell heir to some nice old bits of mahogany, a folding-screen, a matting rug, a mirror, and a pair of white muslin curtains. . . .

Alas! The heat, the smell of the wounds, and close confinement to her rounds brought upon my mother the only illness I could remember, for her muscles and nerves always seemed to be made of iron. It was fortunately brief, and I then took my turn at the same trouble. But our initiation to Camp Winder over, we soon found forgetfulness of discomfort in the awful realities of brave men's suffering on every hand. I followed my mother in her rounds, aiding and supplementing her. Ere long, I found certain patients who in due course were relegated entirely to my care, with a ward helper in attendance. My whole heart passed into the work. I could hardly sleep for wishing to be back in those miserable cheerless wards, where dim eyes would kindle feebly at sight of me and trembling lips gave me last messages to transmit to those they would never see again. Once, going into one of my mother's wards, I found my way blocked by an arm lying on the floor, and the surgeons who had just amputated it and were still at work on Cavanagh, one of our favorite patients, a big, gentle Irishman, always courteous and considerate. The blood was gushing profusely from the flaps they were sewing together, and for a moment I paused uncertain. "Can you stand it?" asked one of the doctors kindly. "If so, there's a little help needed, as we're short-handed this morning." I stayed, and in a moment I saw clear and all seemed easier. When they hurried off, leaving Cavanagh to me, he came out of chloroform looking me full in the eyes, as I stood sponging his forehead. "So it's gone at last, the poor old arm we worked so hard to save," I said, trying to speak lightly. "Yes, miss, but it's not meself you should be thinkin' about," he answered, "an' you standin' by, dirtyin' your dress with the blood o' me." Cavanagh, I am glad to say, got well and left the hospital, swearing eternal fealty to his nurse.

One night, following a day when the cannon had not ceased till sunset, we were awakened by an orderly coming to tell my mother that a lot of new wounded had been brought in from the field and were still coming. They were putting them in a new ward just built at the far end of the camp, but had actually no food or stimulant to give them. Did Mrs. Cary think she could possibly spare a little from her store-room, since many of these poor fellows had been in the ambulance since the day before, some without a mouthful passing their lips?

We sprang up, hurried into our clothes, and were outside in a few minutes. My mother, unlocking her stores with a sinking heart, found she had but one bucket of milk, a small bottle of brandy, a piece of cold boiled pork, and a pile of cold corn-bread. With our arms full, we stumbled in the darkness over the rough ground, following the orderly and his lantern. If we had spilt that precious milk our hearts would have broken then and there!

The Southern night had spent its early heat, and a wandering breeze laden with wood odors came up from the river and smote our foreheads gratefully. At the door of the new ward, a long pine shed, ambulances were disgorging their ghastly contents, some of the wounded uttering pitifully prayers to be left to die in peace, some mercifully in stupor, while other forms were lifted out already stiffened in their last sleep. Those for whom the jolting ride from the battle-field had not finished the work of the enemy's bullets were carried in and laid on the cots, and by the insufficient glimmer of oil lanterns and tallow dips the surgeons began their rounds. Before they were half finished, a streak of saffron came into the sky seen through the open windows, and in the sparse trees on the outskirts of the camp, birds had begun to stir and chirp. We placed our supplies on a table near the door, and my mother, telling me the surgeons needed her assistance, bade me find out the exact number to be fed and "make it go around." Ah! That division of meager portions! Never since, have I been able to endure with complacency seeing the waste of food in peace times. When, aided by the ward helpers, I began to distribute it, some were past swallowing, and their more vigorous neighbors looked with covetous eyes upon the poor rejected bits. To hurry by carrying off these morsels, to take cups away from thirsty lips before they were satisfied, was a keen sorrow.

At length, when I had nearly finished the task and almost exhausted my resources, I came upon a cot where lay upon his face a mere boy apparently dying. There was no time to call a doctor. I mixed milk and brandy, and after forcing his body over poured it by teaspoonfuls down his throat, keeping on till I had the joy of seeing the vital spark creep back. Little by little he reached the point of opening his eyes, and telling me he didn't exactly know what was the matter with him, but that he felt "so tired." As soon as I could capture my favorite doctor, I brought him to my patient. A wound was found, but a slight one. The lad was simply dying from exhaustion, the joggling of hours in the ambulance, and want of food. "He may thank his stars you kept on trying," said my doctor, "or he'd have been a dead one before now. Think of children like this put into the ranks to fill the places of the seasoned men they've killed for us!" . . .

To multiply instances of our work among the sufferers that long, long summer would be monotonous. I depict it as an example of a life led by hundreds of women of the South—women who had mostly come out of beautiful and luxurious homes. My mother, previously a volunteer, was now a paid servant of government, and, of what she received, spent the greater part in amplifying the conveniences and supplies of her diet kitchen. We were then in straits for everything considered indispensable in the outfit of modern hospitals. Our surgeons, working with pure devotion, were at their wits end to renew needful appliances. Without going into painful detail, I can say that our experience was continually shocking and distressing, as were the burials of our dead in a field by Hollywood, six or seven coffins dropped into one yawning pit, and hurriedly covered in, all that a grateful country could render.[8]

Judith McGuire's Diary Continues

Sunday May 8 . . . The fleet upon James River has landed about 30,000 or 40,000 troops. One of their gunboats ran upon a torpedo, which blew it to atoms. We repulsed near Port Walthall. Yesterday they came with a very strong force upon the Petersburg Railroad. . . . The alarm-bell is constantly ringing, making us nervous and anxious. The militia has been called out and has left the city, but where they have gone I know not. It is strange how little apprehension seems to be felt in the city. Our trust is first in God, and, under Him, in our brave men. At this moment Yankee prisoners are passing by. I do not know where they were captured. Those taken at the battle of "The Wilderness" were sent south.

Wednesday, May 11—The last three days have been most exciting. The enemy on the south side of the river have made heavy demonstrations; their force is perhaps 40,000; ours not half that number. The militia, the City Battalion, and the clerks have gone from Richmond. . . . We knew that the attachés of the War Department had received orders to spend the night there, and our son had promised us that if anything exciting occurred he would come up and let us know. We were first aroused by hearing a number of soldiers pass up Broad Street. I sprang up, and saw at least a brigade passing by. As we were composing ourselves to sleep, I heard several pebbles come against the widow. On looking out, I saw J. standing below. In a moment the door was opened and he was in our room, with information brought by a courier that 7,000 raiders were within sixteen miles of us, making their way to the city. He also said 3,000 infantry marched to meet them. Every lady in the house dressed immediately, and some of us went down to the porch. There we saw ladies in every porch, and walking on the pavements, as if it was evening. We saw but one person who seemed really alarmed; everyone else seemed to expect something to occur to stop the raiders. Our city had too often been saved as if by a miracle. About two o'clock a telegram came from General Stewart that he was in pursuit of the enemy. J. came up to bring us the information, and we felt that all was right. In a very short time families had retired to their chambers and quietness reigned in this hitherto perturbed street. For ourselves, we were soon asleep.

May 13—General Stuart died of his wounds last night, twenty-four hours after he was shot. . . . The funeral took place this evening at St. James's Church. My duty to the living prevented my attending it, for which I am very sorry; but I was in the hospital from three o'clock until eight, soothing the sufferers in the only way I could, by fanning them, bathing their wounds, and giving them a word of comfort. . . .

14th— . . . The death of another of our beloved E[piscopal] H[igh] S[chool] boys shocked us greatly. . . . Thus our young men, of the first blood of the country—first in character and education, and what are more important to us now, first in gallantry and patriotism—fall one by one. What a noble army of martyrs has already passed away! I tremble for the future, but we must not think of the future "Sufficient unto the day is the evil thereof."

23rd— . . . At the [General Stuart] funeral—at the head of the coffin—sat the soldier who had rescued him, all battle-stained and soiled; and nearby, the members of his staff, who all adored him. Upon the coffin lay a sword, formed of delicate white flowers, a cross of white roses, and above these the heavenly crown, symbolized by one of green bay-leaves. We followed him to the church, where, after appropriate ceremonies, attended by many people, his body was taken to Hollywood Cemetery. No martial pomp, no soldier's funeral. . . .

May 26—We are now anticipating a fight at Hanover Junction. General Lee fell back to that point on Sunday last, for some good purpose, no doubt. Our army is in the line of battle on the Cedar Hill plantation. The ladies of the family have come to Richmond to avoid the awful collision about to take place. That house, I sadly fear, is to be another sacrifice. Your successes have been wonderful, and evidently, I think, directed by God. We have, however, just met with a sad reverse in Charles City County. . . . Alas, alas for our gallant army! Bravery cannot always contend safely against overwhelming numbers. We are very uneasy about our dear ones who were in that fight. Strange stories are told of the wounded having been bayonetted. It is difficult to believe that men of human hearts could do such things; and while I feel unhappy about the rumor, I cannot credit it.

May 27— . . . We returned to the office yesterday, which was closed for a week. It is pitiable to see how the rations are being reduced by degrees. The Government is exerting itself for the relief of the soldiers. God have mercy upon and help us!

11th—Just heard from W. and S.H. Both places in ruins, except the dwelling houses. Large portions of the Federal army were on them for eight days. S.H. was used as a hospital for the wounded brought from the battlefields; this protected the house. At W. several generals had their head-quarters in the grounds near the house, which, of course, protected it. . . . Dr. B. was at home, with several Confederate wounded from the battle of "Haw's Shop" in the house. Being absent a mile or two from home when they arrived, they so quickly threw out pickets, spread their tents over the surrounding fields and hills that he could not return to his house, where his wife and only child were alone, until he obtained a pass from a Yankee officer. As he approached the house, thousands and tens of thousands of horses and cattle were roaming over the fine wheat fields on his and the adjoining estate, (that of his niece, Mrs. N.) which were now ripe for the sickle. The clover fields and fields of young corn were sharing the same fate. He found his front porch filled with officers. They asked him of his sentiments with regard to the war. He told them frankly that he was an original Secessionist, and ardently hoped to see the North and South separate and distinct nations now and forever. One of them replied that he "honored his candor," and from that moment he was treated with great courtesy. After some difficulty, he was allowed to keep his wounded Confederates, and in one or two instances the federal surgeons assisted him in dressing their wounds. At S.H., the parlor was used for an amputating room, and Yankee blood streamed through that beautiful apartment and the adjoining passage. Poor M. had her stricken heart sorely lacerated in every way, particularly when her son came running in and nestled up to her in alarm. A soldier had asked him, "Are you the son of Captain Newton, who was killed in Culpeper?" "Yes," replied the child. "Well, I belong to the Eighth Illinois, and was one of the soldiers that fired at him when he fell," was the barbarous reply. . . .

July 18th—Since the last note in my diary, we have been pursuing our usual course. The tenor of our way is singularly rough and uneven, marked by the sound of cannon, the marching of troops and all the paraphernalia of grim-visaged war; but we still visit our friends and relatives, and have our pleasant social and family meetings, as though we were at peace with all the world. The theme of every tongue is our army in Maryland. What is it doing? What will be the result of the venture?

July 24ᵗʰ—Amid all the turbulent scenes which surround us, our only grandchild has seen the light and the dear little fellow looks as quiet as though all were peace. We thank God for this precious gift, this little object of all-ascribing interest, which so pleasantly diverts our troubled minds. . . .

The city looks warlike, though the inhabitants are quiet. Troops are constantly passing to and from army wagons, ambulances, etc., rattle by, morning, noon and night. Grant remains passive on the Appomattox [River]. Occasionally throwing a shell into Petersburg, which may probably explode among women and children—but what matters it? They are rebels-what difference does it make about their lives and limbs?

July 27—General Early has returned from Maryland, bringing horses, cattle, etc. While near Washington, the army burned Mr. Montgomery Blair's house which I cannot persuade myself to regret, and spared the residence of his father, by order, it is said, of General Breckinridge. I know that General Breckinridge was right, but I think it required great forbearance, particularly in the soldiers, who have felt in their persons and families the horrors of this cruel war of invasion. It seems our human view that unless the war is severely felt by those in high authority, it will never cease. . . . There seems to be no pity in the hearts of many of the Federal generals. Women and children are made homeless at midnight, and not allowed to save anything, even their clothes. When houses are not burned, they are robbed of everything which a precious soldiery may desire. The last barrel of flours, the last ham, is taken from store-rooms; and this is done, not in Virginia only; . . . But poor old Virginia has been furrowed and scarred until her original likeness is gone. . . . Marked by a hundred battle-fields, and checked by fortifications, almost every spot is classic ground. From the beginning she has acted her part nobly, and has already covered herself with glory; but when the war is over, where shall we find her old churches, where her noble homesteads, scenes of domestic comfort and generous hospitality? Either laid low by the firebrand, or desecrated and desolated. In the march of the army, or in the rapid evolutions of raiding parties, woe betides the houses which are found deserted! In many cases the families of men having gone to war, the women and children dare not stay; then the lawless are allowed to plunder. They seem to take the greatest delight in breaking up the most elegant or the most humble furniture, as the case may be; cut the portraits from the frames, split pianos in pieces, ruin libraries, in any way that suites their fancy; break doors from hinges, and locks from the doors; cut the windows from their frames, and leave no pane of glass unbroken; carry off house-linens and carpets; the contents of store-rooms and pantries, sugar, flour, vinegar, molasses, pickles, preserves, which cannot be eaten or carried off, are poured together in one general mass; the horses are of course taken from the stables; cattle and stock of all kinds driven off or shot in the woods and fields. Generally, indeed, I believe always when the whole army is moving, inhabited houses are protected. To the raiders such as Hunter and Co. is reserved the credit for committing such outrages in the presence of ladies—of taking their watches from their belts, their rings from their fingers, and their ear-rings from their ears; of searching their bureau and wardrobes, and filling pockets and haversacks in their presence. Is it not then wonderful that soldiers whose families have suffered such things could be restrained when in a hostile country? It seems to me to show a marvelous degree of forbearance in the officers themselves, and of discipline in the troops.

August 11—Sheridan's and Early's troops are fighting in the Valley. We suffered a disaster near Martinsburg, and all our troops fell back to Strasburg; had a fight on the old battlefield at Kernstown, and we drove the enemy through Winchester to Martinsburg, which our troops took possession of; Port Winchester, how checkered its history throughout the war! Abounding with patriotism as it is, what a blessing it must be to have a breath of free air, even though it be for a short time! Their welcome of our soldiers is always so joyous, so bounding, so generous! How they must enjoy the blessed privilege of speaking their own sentiments without having their servants listening and acting as spies in their houses, and of being able to hear from or write to their friend! Oh! I would that there was a prospect of their being disenthralled forever.

12^(th)— . . . One of my friends in the office is a victim of Millroy's reign in Winchester. She wrote to a friend of hers at the North, expressing her feelings rather imprudently. The letter was intercepted, and she was immediately arrested, and brought in an ambulance through the enemy's lines to our picket-post, where she was deposited by the roadside. She says that she was terribly distressed at leaving her mother and sisters, but when she got into Confederate lines the air seemed wonderfully fresh, pure and free, and she soon found friends. She came to Richmond and entered our office. About the same time a mother and daughters who lived perhaps in the handsomest house in the town, were arrested, for some alleged imprudence of one of the daughters. An ambulance was driven to the door, and the mother was taken from her sick-bed and put into it, together with the daughters. Time was not allowed for them to prepare a lunch for the journey. Before Mrs.—was taken from her house, Mrs. Millroy had entered it, the General having taken it for his head-quarters; and before the ambulance had been driven off, one of their own officers was heard to say to Mrs. Millroy, seeing her so entirely at home in the house, "For goodness' sake, madam, wait until the poor women gets off." Is it wonderful, then, that the Winchester ladies welcome our troops with gladness? That they rush out and join the band, singing "The bonnie blue flag" and "Dixie" as the troops entered the streets, until their enthusiasm and melody melt all hearts? Was it strange that even the great and glorious, though grave and thoughtful, Stonewall Jackson should, when pursuing Banks through its streets, have been excited until he waved his cap with tears of enthusiasm, as they broke forth in harmonious songs of welcome? Or that the ladies, not being satisfied by saluting them with their voices, waving their handkerchiefs, and shouting for joy, should follow them with more substantial offerings, filling their haversacks with all their depleted pantries could afford? Or is it wonderful that our soldiers should love Winchester so dearly and fight for it so valiantly? No, it is beautiful to contemplate the long-suffering, the firmness under oppression, the patience, the generosity, the patriotism of Winchester. Other towns, I dare say, have borne the tyranny as well, and when their history is known they will call forth our admiration as much; but we *know* of no such instance. The "Valley" throughout shows the same devotion to our cause, and the sufferings of the country people are even greater than those in town.

Some amusing incidents sometimes occur, showing the eagerness of the ladies to serve our troops after a long separation. A lady living near Berryville but a little remote from the main road, says, that when our troops are passing through the country, she sometimes feels sick with anxiety to do something for them. She, one morning, stood in her porch, and could see them turn in crowds to neighboring houses which happened to be on the road, but no one turned out of the way far enough to come to her house. At last one man came along, and finding that he was passing her gate, she ran out with great alacrity to invite him to come in to get his breakfast. He turned to her with an amused expression and replied; "I am much obliged to you, madam; I wish I could breakfast with you, but as I have already eaten four breakfasts to please the ladies, I must beg you to excuse me."

14th—Norfolk, poor Norfolk! Nothing can exceed its long suffering, its nights of gloom and darkness. Unlike Winchester, it has no bright spots—no oasis in its blank desert of wretchedness. Like Alexandria, it has no relief, but must submit, and drag on its chain of servility, till the final cry of victory bursts its bonds, and makes it free. I have no time to write all I hear and know of the indignities offered to our countrymen and countrywomen in Alexandria, Norfolk, Portsmouth, and other places, which remain incarcerated in the sloughs of Federal tyranny. God help them, and give us strength speedily to break the chain that binds them.

August 22d—Just been on a shopping expedition for my sister and niece, and spent $1,500 in about an hour. I gave $110 for ladies morocco boots; $22 per yard for linen; $5 apiece for spools of cotton; $5 for a paper of pins, etc. It would be utterly absurd, except that it is melancholy, to see our currency depreciating so rapidly.

31st—The last day of this exciting, troubled summer of 1864. How many young spirits have fled; how many bleeding hearts have been left upon earth, from the sanguinary work of this summer! Grant still remains near Petersburg; still by that means is he besieging Richmond. He has been baffled at all points, and yet his indomitable perseverance knows no bounds. Sherman still besieges Atlanta. God help us!

We are again troubled in mind and body about engaging rooms; we find we must give up these by the 1st of October, and have begun the usual refugee occupation of room-hunting.

Letters from our friends in the Valley, describing the horrors now going on there. . . . During the same night the pickets near to other large houses were fired on. This being reported at head-quarters, the order was at once issued to burn all three houses. Two companies of the Fifth Michigan cavalry, commanded by Captain Drake, executed the fearful order. They drew up in front of Mr.—'s house and asked him "Are you Mr.—?" demanded the Captain. "I have orders to burn your house." In vain, Mr.—remonstrated. He begged for one hour, that he might see General Custer and explain the circumstances of the night before; he also pleaded the illness of his son-in-law, then in the house. No reply was vouchsafed to the old gentlemen, but with a look of hardened ferocity, he turned to address the soldiers, with the order: "Men, to your work, and do it thoroughly." In an instant the torch was applied to that house of domestic elegance and comfort. One soldier seized the sick son-in-law, who is a surgeon in our service, threatening to carry him to our head-quarters, and was with difficulty prevented by the kind interposition of Dr. Sinclair, the surgeon of the regiment. They allowed the family to save as much furniture as they could, but the servants were all gone and there was no one near to help them. The soldiers at once went to Mr.—'s secretary, containing $40,000 in bonds, destroyed it, and scattered the mutilated papers to the winds. Matches were applied to window and bed curtains; burning coals were sprinkled in the linen-closet, containing every variety of house and table linen. Mrs.—, the daughter, opened a drawer, and taking her jewelry, embracing an elegant diamond ring and other valuables, was escaping with them to the yard, when she was seized by two ruffians on the stair-steps, held by the arms of one, while the other forcibly took the jewels; they then, as she was very small woman, lifted her over the banister and let her drop into the passage below; fortunately it was not very far and she was not at all injured. Nothing daunted, she rushed up-stairs, to rescue a box containing her bridal presents of silver, which was concealed in the wall above a closet. She climbed up to the highest shelf of the closet, seized the box, and with unnatural strength, threw it through the window into the yard below. While still on the shelf, securing other things from their hiding-place, all unconscious of danger, as soldier set fire to some dresses hanging of the pegs below the shelf on which she stood. The first intimation she had of it was feeling the heat; she then leaped over the flames to the floor; her stockings were scorched, but she was not injured. She next saw a man with the sign of the Cross on his coat; she asked him if he was a chaplain? He replied that he was. She said, "Then in mercy come, and help me save some of my mother's things." They went into her mother's chamber, and she hurriedly opened the bureau drawer, and began taking out the clothes, the chaplain assisting, but what was to her horror to see him putting whatever he fancied into his pocket—among other things a paper of pins. She says she could not help saying, as she turned to him, "A minister of Christ stealing pins!!" In a moment the chaplain was gone, but the pins were returned to the bureau. Mrs.—is the only daughter of Mr.—, and was the only lady on the spot. Her first care, when she found the house burning, was to secure her baby, which was sleeping in its cradle up-stairs. A guard was at the foot of the steps, and refused to let her pass; she told him that she was going to rescue her child from the flames. "Let the little d—d rebel burn!" was the brutal reply. But his bayonet could not stop her; she ran by and soon returned, bearing her child to a place of safety. When the house had become a heap of ruins, the mother returned to the bedside of her dead sister, whither she had gone at daybreak that morning, on horseback, (for her harness had been destroyed by the enemy, making her carriage useless.) She was, of course, overwhelmed with grief and with horror at the scene before her. As soon as she dismounted, a soldier leaped on the horse, and rode off with it. Their work of destruction in one place being now over, they left it for another scene of vengeance.

The same ceremony of Captain Drake's announcing his orders to the mistress of the mansion (the master was a prisoner) being over, the torch was applied. The men had dismounted; the work of pillage was going on merrily; the house was burning in every part, to insure total destruction. The hurried tramp of horses' feet could not be heard amidst the crackling of flames and falling of rafters, but the sudden shout and cry of "No quarter! No quarter!" from many voices resounded in the ears of the unsuspecting marauders as a death-knell. A company of Mosby's men rushed up the hill and charged them furiously; they were aroused by the sound of danger, and fled hither and thither. Terrified and helpless, they were utterly unprepared for resistance. The cry of "No quarter! No quarter!"

still continued. They hid behind the burning ruins; they crouched in the corners of fences; they begged for life; but their day of grace was past. The defenseless women, children, and old men of the neighborhood had borne their tortures too long; something must be done, and all that this one company of braves could do, was done. Thirty were killed on the spot, and others, wounded and bleeding, sought refuge, and asked pity of those whom were endeavoring to ruin. . . .

Such are some of the horrors that are being enacted in Virginia at this time. These among many, many others, I note in my diary. . . .

10th—We must give up our rooms by the last of this month, and the question now arises about our future abode. We are searching hither and thither. We had thought for a week past that our arrangements were most delightfully made, and we had procured, together with Dr. M. and Colonel G., six rooms in a house on Franklin Street. The arrangements had been made, and the proprietor gone from town. The M.'s and ourselves were to take four rooms in the third story; the back parlor on the first floor was to be used by all parties; and Colonel G. would take the large front basement room as his chamber, and at his request, as our dining-room, as we could not be allowed to use the upper chambers as eating-rooms. Our large screen was transferred to the Colonel's bedstead and washing apparatus, and the rest of the room furnished in dining-room style. These rooms were all furnished and carpeted. Nothing could have suited us better, and we have been for some days anticipating our comfortable winter-quarters. The M.'s have left town with the blissful assurance of a nice home; to add to it all, the family of the proprietor is all we could desire as friends and companions. Last night I met with a friend, who asked me where we had obtained rooms. I described to them with great alacrity and pleasure. She looked surprised, and said, "Are you not mistaken? Those rooms are already occupied." "Impossible." said I; "We have engaged them." She shook her head, saying, "There must be some mistake; they have been occupied for some days by a family, who say that they have rented them." No person situated exactly in the same way can imagine our disappointment. The Colonel looked aghast; Mr.—pronounced it a mistake; the girls were indignant and I went a little farther, and pronounced it bad treatment. This morning I went up before breakfast to hear the truth of the story—the family is still absent, but the servants confirmed the statement by saying that a family had been in the rooms that we looked at for a week, and a gentleman, a third party, had been up the day before to claim the rooms, and said that the party occupying them had no right to them, and must be turned out. The servant added that this third gentleman had sent up a dray with flour, which was now in the house and had put his coal in the coal-cellar. All this seems passing strange. Thus we have but three weeks before us in which to provide ourselves with an almost impossible shelter. The "Colonel" has written to Mr.—for an explanation, and the M.'s have been apprised of their dashed hopes. I often think how little the possessors of the luxurious homes of Richmond know of the difficulties with which the refugees are surrounded, and how little we ever appreciated the secure home-feeling which we had all enjoyed before the war began. We have this evening been out again in pursuit of quarters. The advertisements of "Rooms to let" were sprinkled over the morning papers; so that one could scarcely believe that there would be difficulty in our being supplied. A small house that would accommodate our whole party, five or six rooms in a large house, or two rooms for ourselves, if it were impossible to do better, would answer our purpose—any thing for a comfortable home. The first advertisement alluded to basement rooms—damp, and redolent of rheumatism. The next more attractive—good rooms, well furnished and up but two flights of stairs; but the price was enormous, far beyond the means of any of the party, and so evidently an extortion designed to take all that could be extracted from the necessity of others, that we turned from our hard-featured proprietor with disgust. The rooms of the third advertisement had already been rented, and the fourth seemed more like answering our purpose than any we had seen. There were only two rooms, and though small, and rather dark, yet persons whose shelter was likely to be the "blue vault of heaven" could not be very particular. The price, too, was exorbitant, but with a little more self-denial it might be paid. The next inquiry was about kitchen, servant's room and coal-house; but we got no further than the answer about the kitchen. The lady said there was no kitchen that we could possibly use; her stove was small and she required it all. We must either be supplied from a restaurant, or do our own cooking in one of the rooms. As neither plan is to be thought of, we ended the parley. Apart from a kitchen that is indispensible, though perhaps the most annoying thing to which refugees are subjected. The mistress is generally polite enough, but save me from the self-sufficient cook. "I would like to oblige you, madam, but you can't have loaf-bread to-morrow morning, because my mistress has ordered loaf-bread and rolls, and our stove is small;" or "No madam, you can't 'bile a ham, nor nothing else to-day, because it is our washing-day;" or, "No, ma'am, you can't have biscuits for tea, because the stove is cold, and I've got no time to heat it." So that we must either submit, or go to the mistress for redress, and probably find none, and thus run the risk of offending both mistress and maid, both of whom have us very much in their power. As I walked home from this unsuccessful effort, it is nearly dark; the gas was being lighted in hall, parlor, and chamber. I looked in as I passed, and saw cheerful countenances collecting around centre-tables, or sitting here and there on handsome porticos or marble steps to enjoy the cool evening breeze—countenances of those whose families I had known from infancy, and who were still numbered among my friends and acquaintances. I felt sad, and asked myself, if those persons could realize the wants of others, would not cheerfully rent some of their extra rooms? Rooms once opened on grand occasions, and now, as occasions are few and far between, not opened at all for weeks and months together.

Would they not cheerfully remove some of their showy and fragile furniture for a time, and, allow those who had once been accustomed to as large rooms of their own to occupy and take care of them? The rent would perhaps be no object with them, but their kindness might be twice blessed—the refugees would be made comfortable and happy, and the money might be applied to the wants of the soldiers or the city poor. And yet a third blessing might be added—the luxury of doing good. Ah, they would find that the "quality of mercy is not strained," but it would be indeed, like the "gentle dew from heaven," fall into their very souls, and diffuse a happiness of which they know not. These thoughts filled my mind until I reached the present home of a refugee friend from Washington. It was very late, but I thought I would run in, and see if she could throw any light upon our difficulties. I was sorry to find that she was in a similar situation, her husband having that day been notified that their rooms would be required on the first of October. We compared notes of our room-hunting experiences and conversation which were both provoking and ridiculous. I then wended my way home, amid brilliantly lighted houses and badly lighted streets. Squads of soldiers were sauntering along, impregnating the air with tobacco-smoke; men were standing at every corner, lamenting the fall of Atlanta or the untimely end of General

Morgan. I too often caught a word, conveying blame of the President for having removed General Johnston. This blame always irritates me, because the public became so impatient at General Johnston's want of action, that they were clamorous for his removal. For weeks the President was abused without measure because he was not removed, and now the same people are using the same terms towards him because the course which they absolutely required at his hands has disappointed them. The same people a month ago curled the lip in scorn at General Johnston's sloth and want of energy, and praised General Hood's course from the beginning of the war, now shrug their unmilitary shoulders, who straps have never graced a battlefield, and pronounce the change "unfortunate and uncalled for." General Hood, they say, was an "admirable Brigadier" but his "promotion was most unfortunate," while General Johnston's "Fabian Policy" is now pronounced the very thing for the "situation" the course which would have saved Atlanta, and have made all right. This may be all true, but it is very distressing to hear it harped upon now; quite as much so as it was six weeks ago to hear the President called obstinate, because he was ruing the country by not removing General J. But I will no longer make myself uneasy about what I hear for I have implicit confidence in our leaders, both in the Cabinet and on the field. Were I a credulous woman, ready to believe all that I hear in the office, in the hospital, in my visits and on the streets, I should think that Richmond is now filled with the most accomplished military geniuses on which the sun shines. Each man expresses himself, as an old friend would say, with the most "dogmatic infallibility" of the conduct of the President, General Lee, General Johnston, General Hampton, General Beauregard, General Wise, together with all the other lights of every degree. It is true that there are as many varieties of opinion as there are men expressing them, or I should profoundly regret that so much military light should be obscured among the shades of Richmond departments; but I do wish that some of them would refrain from condemning the acts of our leaders, and from uttering such awful prophecies, provided the President or General Lee does not do so and so. Although I do not believe their forebodings, yet the reiteration of such opinions, in the most assured tones, makes me nervous and uneasy. I would that all such men be sent to the field; I think at least a regiment could be spared from Richmond, for then the women of the city at least would be more peaceful.

12th— . . . The morning papers report "all quiet" at Petersburg, except that shells are daily thrown into the city, and that many of the women and children are living in tents in the country, so as to be out of reach of shells.

General Hood telegraphs that the inhabitants of Atlanta have been ordered to leave their homes, to go they know not whither. Lord, how long must we suffer such things? I pray that the enemy's hands may be stayed, and that they may be driven from our fair borders to their own land. I ask not vengeance upon them, but they may be driven to their own homes, and that we may be henceforward and forever a separate people.

16th—A visit to-day from my brother Dr. B., who bears the utter desolation of his home quietly, through so sudden a change of circumstances is of course very depressing. He tells me that he has lately had a visit from a very interesting young South Carolinian, who came to look for the body of his brother. The two brothers being educated in Germany when the war broke out; and as soon as they were of military age, with the consent of their parents, they hastened home to take part in their country's struggle. In one of the cavalry fights in Hanover, in May last, one brother was killed, and the other, "not being able to find the body at the time, was now seeking it." His mother was on the ocean returning to her home, and he could not meet her with the information that her son's body could not be found. He had heard that some of the fallen had been buried at S.H. or W. He mentioned that their intimate friend, young Middleton, had fallen in the same fight. Mr. Middleton had been buried at S. H. and his grave had been marked by Mrs. N.; but young Pringle (the name of the brothers) had been carried to neither place. Mr. Pringle had seen in a New York paper an account given by a Yankee officer of several wounded Confederates, who had been captured, and having died on their way to the "White House," they were buried by the roadside, and he had some reason to believe that his brother was among them. It was then remembered that there were three graves on the opposite side of the Pamunky River, and one was marked with the name "Tingle". It was an excessively warm Sunday morning; but as the young soldier's furlough only extended to the following day, there was no time to be lost. Dr. B. and the brother set out upon their melancholy mission, having obtained a cart, one or two men, and given an order at a neighboring carpenter's shop for a coffin. After crossing the river they found the three graves, at the place designated, in the county of King William. The one marked "Tingle" contained the body of a federal and one of a Confederate soldier but not the brother. The next one opened was not the right one; but the third contained the much-loved remains, which were easily recognized by the anxious brother. Tenderly and gently, all wrapped in his blanket, he was transferred from his shallow grave to his soldier's coffin, and then conveyed to S. H. to be placed by his friend Middleton. It was now night, the moon shone brightly, and all was ready. The families from both houses gathered around the grave. "Slowly and sadly they laid him down." No minister of the Gospel was near to perform the services. Dr. B. stood at the head with a Prayer-Book for the purpose, but his defective sight obliged him to yield the book to Mrs. N., who, with a clear, calm voice but the light of a single lantern the beautiful ritual of the Episcopal Church. The grave was filled in solemn silence, the brother standing at the foot. When all was over, the young ladies and children of the families advanced with wreaths and bouquets, and in an instant the soldier's grave was a mound of fresh flowers. The brother could no longer restrain his feelings; he was completely overwhelmed, and was obligated to retire to his room, where he could indulge them freely. Next morning he returned to his command, after a leave-taking in which the feelings expressed by all parties evinced more the friendship of years than the acquaintance of hours. It was strange indeed that this scene, so similar to that of the burial of the lamented Captain Latane, should have occurred at the same place. But who could relate, who could number the sad scene of this war? Many such have probably occurred in various parts of the country.

18th—Nothing yet from Mr.—about our rooms. All the furnished rooms that I have seen, except those, would cost us from $100 to $110 per month for each room, which, of course, we cannot pay; but we will try and not be anxious overmuch, for the Lord has never let us want comforts since we left our own dear home, and if we use the means which He has given us properly and in his Fear, He will not desert us now.

I went with Mr.—as usual this morning to the "Officers Hospital" where he read a part of the service and delivered an address to such patients among the soldiers who were well enough to attend. I acted as his chorister, and when the services were over, and he went around to the bedsides of the patients, I crossed the street, as I have done several times before, to the cemetery—the old "Shockoe Hill Cemetery." It is, to me, the most interesting spot in the city. It is a melancholy thought that, after an absence of thirty years, I am almost a stranger in my native place. In the cemetery, I go from spot to spot, and find the names that were the household words of my childhood and youth; the names of my father's and mother's friends; of the friends of my sisters and my own school-days. . . . Time would fail me to enumerate all the loved and lost. Their graves look so peaceful in that lovely spot. Most of them died before the war came to distress them. . . .

But enough of the past and of sadness. I must now turn to busy life again, and note a little victory, of which General Lee telegraphed yesterday, by which we gained some our hundred prisoners, many horses and wagons, and 2,500 beeves. These last are most acceptable to our commissariat!

The Southern Army is having an armistice of ten days, for the inhabitants of Atlanta to get off from their homes. Exiled by Sherman, my heart bleeds for them. May the good Lord have mercy upon them, and have them in His holy keeping!

21ˢᵗ—Bad news this morning. General Early has had a defeat in the Valley, near Winchester, and has fallen back to Strasburg. Our losses reported heavy. . . .

28ᵗʰ—Mr. P. came home, and at once decided that we were entitled to the rooms. By this arrangement we are greatly relieved. The family who occupied them has moved off, and Mr.—having convinced the third party of his mistake has taken off his hands the coal and flour which he had stored away, and now it is all straight. The "Colonel" and ourselves moved our goods and chattels to these rooms yesterday. The M.'s will be here in a day or two. We have a long walk to our offices, but it is very near my hospital. Mr.—'s hospital is very far from every point, as it is on the outskirts of the city; but he thinks the walk is conducive to his health, so that we are, upon the whole, very comfortable.

October 10—I am cast down by hearing that J. P. has been captured; he was caught while scouring in the enemy's lines on James River. Poor child!

I feel very, very anxious about him. Poor army in the Valley has regained its foothold, the enemy having retreated. . . .

The Federal Army below Richmond advanced a few days ago, and took "Fort Harrison." We live now amid perpetual firing of cannon. The loss of Fort Harrison is, I am afraid, a very serious loss to us. . . .

12th—The armies around Richmond remain quiet . . . The hospitals are full of the wounded; my afternoons are very much engaged, nursing them. . . .

November 13— . . . In the Valley of Virginia an immense amount of private property has been destroyed. Sheridan, glorifying in his shame, boasts of, and probably magnifies, what has been done in that way. He telegraphs to Grant that he has burned 2,000 barns. The Lord shortens his dreadful work, and will have mercy upon the sufferers! . . .

The war news seems encouraging. Many persons are very despondent, but I do not feel so—perhaps I do not understand the military signs. Our men below Richmond have certainly had many successes of late. . . .

23rd— . . . Sherman is moving across Georgia in the direction of Milledgeville, looking towards Savannah, or Charleston. . . . Nothing equal to the demands of these trying times have yet been done by any of the authorities. Oh that they would strain every nerve to put a stop to this bold and desolating invader! It would require united effort, made without delay. No hesitation, no doubting and holding back must there be; every human being capable of bearing arms must fly to the rescue; all their stores of every kind should be destroyed or removed; bridges burned, roads torn up or obstructed; every difficulty should be thrown in the way. He should be harassed day and night, that he might be delayed, and entrapped, and ruined. Oh, that these things could be done! It may be a woman's thought, but I believe that had Georgia one tithe of the experience of the ruined, homeless Virginians, she would exert every fiber of her frame to destroy the enemy; she would have no delusive hope of escape. I trust that . . . the people of patriotic Georgia have not been rendered unfit for the sacrifices and dangers of this fearful day, when every man is required to stand in the deadly breach, and every earthly interest, even life itself, must be surrendered rather than yield to the barbarous foe, by their treasonable doctrines of reconstruction, reunion, etc. Oh, I trust not; and I hope that our now uncertain mails bring information that all Georgia and South Carolina are aroused to their awful condition.

17th—The military movements are important, but to what they tend we know not. More troops have been added from Sheridan to Grant, and Early to Lee, and Sherman has crossed Georgia with little opposition or loss. . . .

24th—Savannah has been evacuated, without loss to us, except of some stores, which could not be removed. The city was surrendered by its mayor, Arnold by name, and he seems to be worthy of the traitorous name. Our troops marched towards Charleston. Savannah was of little use to us for a year past; it has been closely blocked, and its surrender relieves troops which were there for its defense, which may be more useful else ware; but the moral effect of its fall is dreadful. The enemy is encouraged, and our people depressed. I never saw them more so. . . .

26th—The sad Christmas has passed away. J. and C. were with us, and very cheerful. We exerted ourselves to be so too. The church services were sweet and comforting. St Paul's was dressed most elaborately and beautifully with evergreens; all looked as usual; but there is much sadness on account of the failure of the South to keep Sherman back. When we got home our family circle was small, but pleasant. The Christmas turkey and ham were not. We had aspired to a turkey, but finding the prices range from $50 to $100 in the market on Saturday, we contented ourselves with roast-beef and the various little dishes which Confederate times have made us believe are tolerable substitutes for the viands of better days. At night, I treated our little party to tea and ginger cakes—two very rare indulgences; and but for the sorghum, grown in our fields, the cakes would be an impossible indulgence. Nothing but the well ascertained fact that Christmas comes but once a year would make such extravagance at all excusable. We propose to have a family gathering when the girls come home, on the day before or after New Year's day, (as that day will come on Sunday,) to enjoy together, and with one or two refugee friends, the contents of the box sent the girls by a young officer who captured it from the enemy, consisting of white sugar, raisins, preserves, pickles, spices, etc.

They threaten to give us a plum-cake, and I hope that they will carry it out, particularly if we have any of our army friends with us. Poor fellows, how they enjoy our plain dinners when they come, and how we love to see them enjoy them! Two meals a day has become the universal system among the refugees, and many citizens, from necessity. The want of our accustomed tea or coffee is very much felt by the elders. The rule with us is only to have tea when sickness makes it necessary, and the headaches gotten up to about dark have become the joke of the family. A country lady, from one of the few spots in all Virginia where the enemy has never been, and consequently where they retain their comforts, asked me gravely why we did not substitute milk for tea. She could scarcely believe me when I told her that we had not milk more than twice in eighteen months, and then it was sent by a country friend. It is now $4 a quart.

28th— . . . Yesterday we had a pleasant little dinner-party at Dr. G.'s—so rare a thing now, that I must note it in my diary. Many nice things on the table were sent by country friends. What would we do without our country friends? Their hearts seem warm and generous to those who are not so well off as themselves. They set a good example, which I trust will not be lost on us. Our relatives and friends, though they have been preyed upon by the enemy almost to exhaustion, never seem to forget us. Sausages from one, a piece of beef from another, a bushel of dried fruit, a turkey, etc., come ever and anon to our assistance. One can scarcely restrain tears of affection, when it is remembered that these things are evidences of self-denial, and not given from their abundance, as at the beginning of the war. The soldiers are not forgotten by these country friends. Those who remember the refugees are never forgetful of the soldiers. Take our people as a whole; they are full of generosity and patriotism. The speculators and money-makers of these trying times are a peculiar class, of which I neither like to speak, think, nor write; they are objects of my implacable disgust. They do not belong to our noble Southern patriots. They are with us, but not of us! I should think that a man who had made a fortune during the war would, when the war is over, wish to hide it, and not own his ill-gotten gains. I trust there are not many such. The year 1864 has almost passed away. Oh, what a fearful account it has rendered to heaven! What calamities and sorrows crowd into its history, in this afflicted country of ours God help us, and guide us onward and upward, for the Savior's sake!

CHAPTER SIX

1865—The War Continues

"Every thing seems so dark and uncertain that I have no heart for keeping records."—Judith McGuire

Judith McGuire's Diary Continues

2d—This bitter cold morning, when we entered the office, we found that our good "Major" had provided us a New Year's treat of hot coffee. Of course, we all enjoyed it highly, and were very grateful to him; and when I returned home, the first thing that met my eye was a box sent from the express office. We opened it, and found it a Christmas box, filled with nice and substantial things from a friend now staying in Buckingham County, for whom I once had an opportunity of doing some trifling kindness; The Lord is certainly taking care of us through His people. The refugees in some of the villages are much worse off than we are. We hear amusing stories of a friend in an inland place, where nothing can possibly be bought, *hiring a skillet from a servant for one dollar* per month, and other cooking utensils, which are absolutely necessary, at the same rate; another in the same village, whose health seems to require that she should drink something *hot* at night, has been obligated to resort to *hot water,* as she has neither tea, coffee, sugar nor milk. These ladies belong to wealthy Virginian families. Many persons have no meat on their tables for months at a time; and they are the real patriots, who submit patiently, and without murmuring, to any privation, provided the country is doing well. The flesh-pots of Egypt have no charms for them; they look forward hopefully to the time when their country shall be disenthralled, never caring for the trials of the past or the present, provided they can hope for the future.

8th—Some persons in this beleaguered city seem crazed on the subject of gayety. In the midst of the wounded and dying, the low state of the commissariat, the anxiety of the whole country, the troubles of every kind by which we are surrounded, I am mortified to say that there are gay parties given in the city. There are those denominated 'Starvation parties" where young persons meet for innocent enjoyment, and retire at a reasonable hour; but there are others when the most elegant suppers are served—cakes, jellies, ices in profusion, and meats of the finest kinds in abundance, such as might furnish a meal for a regiment of General Lee's army. I wish these things were not so, and that every extra pound of meat could be sent to the army. When returning from the hospital, after witnessing the dying scene of a brother, whose young sister hung over him in agony; with my heart full of sorrows of hospital-life, I passed a house where there were music and dancing. The revulsion of feeling was sickening. I thought of the gayety of Paris during the French Revolution, of the "Cholera ball" in Paris, the ball at Brussels the night before the battle of Waterloo, and felt shocked that our own Virginians, at such a time, should remind me of scenes which we were wont to think only belonged to the lightness of foreign society. It seemed to me that the army, when it hears of the gayety of Richmond, must think it heartless, particularly while it is suffering such hardships in her defense. The weddings, of which there are many, seem to be conducted with great quietness. . . . There seems to be a perfect mania on the subject of matrimony. Some of the churches may be seen open and lighted almost every night for A soldier in our hospital called to me as I passed his bed the other day, "I say, Mrs.——, when do you think my wound will be well enough for me to go to the country?" "Before very long, I hope." "But what does the doctor say, for I am mighty anxious to go?" I looked at his disabled limb and talked to him of his being able to enjoy the country air in a short time. "Well, try to get me up, for, you see, it ain't the country air I am after, but I wants to get married, and the lady don't know that I am wounded, maybe she'll think I don't want to come." "Ah." said I, "but you must show her your scars, and if she is a girl worth having she will love you all the better for having bled for your country; and you must tell her that "It is always the heart that is bravest in war, that is fondest and truest in love."

He looked perfectly delighted with the idea; and as I passed him again he called out, "Lady, please stop a minute and tell me the verse over again, for, you see, when I do get there, if she is affronted, I wants to give her the prettiest excuse I can, and I think that the verse is beautiful."

Social Life in Richmond

. . . During the war Richmond had happy phases for its social life. Entertainments were given very freely and very liberally the first year of the war and at them suppers were generously furnished but as the war progressed all this was of necessity given up and we had instead "starvation parties".

The young ladies of the city, accompanied by their male escorts (generally Confederate soldiers on leave) would assemble at a fashionable residence that before the war had been the abode of wealth, and have music and plenty of dancing, but not a morsel of food or a drop of drink was seen. And this form of entertainment became the popular and universal one in Richmond. Of course no food or wine was served simply because they could not get it, or could not afford it. At these starvation parties the young people of Richmond and the young army officers assembled and danced as brightly and as happily as though a supper worthy of Lucullus awaited them.

The ladies were simply dressed, many of them without jewelry, because the women of the South had given their jewelry to the Confederate cause. Often, on the occasion of these starvation parties, some young southern girl would appear in an old gown belonging to her mother or grand-mother, or possibly a still more remote ancestor, And the effect of the antique garment was very peculiar; but no matter what was worn, no matter how peculiarly any one might be attired, no matter how bad the music, no matter how limited the host's or hostess's ability to entertain, everyone laughed, danced, and was happy, although the reports of the cannon often boomed in their ears, and all deprivation, all deficiencies were looked on as a sacrifice to the southern cause.

The condition of the Allen household was that of all Richmond. *(ed.—Mr. and Mrs. Allen are shown in front of their house in the Pictures section.)* Sometimes the contrasts that occurred in these social gayeties in Richmond were frightful, ghastly. A brilliant, handsome, happy, joyous young officer, full of hope and promise, would dance with a lovely girl, and return to his command; a few days would elapse, another starvation party would occur; the officer would be missed, he would be asked for, and the reply came, "Killed in battle;" and frequently the same girls with whom he had danced a few nights before would attend his funeral from one of the churches in Richmond. Can life have any more terrible antithesis than this?

On one occasion when I was attending a starvation party in Richmond the dancing was at its height and everyone was bright and happy, when the hostess, who was a widow, was suddenly called out of the room. A hush fell on everything, the dancing stopped, and everyone became sad, all having a premonition in these troublous times that something fearful had happened. We were soon told that her son had been killed later that evening in a skirmish in front of Richmond, a few miles from his home. . . .

Private theatricals were also a form of amusement during the war. I saw several of them. The finest I witnessed, however, was a performance of Sheridan's comedy, The Rivals, in which that brilliant lady, Mrs. Senator Clay, of Alabama, played Mrs. Malaprop. Her rendition was one of the best I ever saw, rivaling that of any professional. The audience was very brilliant. The President of the Confederacy, Mr., Davis, Judah P. Benjamin, and others of equal distinction were present.

Mr. Davis, at the Executive Mansion, held weekly receptions, to which the public was admitted. These continued until nearly the end of the war. The occasions were not especially marked but Mr. Davis and Mrs. Davis were always delightful hosts.[9]

At levees, receptions and at the simple teas—which the high toned disparaged for being too informal; and democratic—Varina Davis labored mightily to please her husband's associates. Constant Cary, a reigning belie of Confederate society, perhaps best understood the first lady's character. She described her as warmhearted and impetuous, witty and thin skinned—a complex combination of strengths and weaknesses. [10]

The pursuit of pleasure seemed to mock the heroic sacrifices of soldier and civilian alike. "If Spartan austerity is to win our independence, we are lost as a nation. I do not like the signs and fear the writing on the wall might in time come to us." Phoebe Pember warned. Sensitive women could hardly enjoy a dance or reception without thinking about their husbands, brothers, and sweethearts in danger. Of course, the pious had always frowned on frivolous entertainment, but the war added new force to their arguments and even made some young people unusually sober minded.[11]

But Southern society had always been divided between a church-based popular culture and a more secular and extravagant upper-class culture. The war only intensified the conflict between self-restraint and hedonistic indulgence. For members of the Southern elite torn between these competing ideals, the best solution seemed to have it both ways. Wealthy Richmond women sewed and knitted for the soldiers. Even austerity could be ostentatious and public patriotism might obscure less-elevated motives. Constance Cary and other young women held "starvation parties" at which no refreshments were served. The music, dancing and tableau vivants provided entertainments for the soldiers (generally officers) and made women who usually dined in style feel that they had given up something for the cause. . . . In June 1863, only two months after the Richmond bread riot, Phoebe Pember attended a party with the Cary sisters and a bevy of local belles where she ate strawberries and ice cream and promenaded with some handsome cavaliers.[12]

Judith McGuire Diary Continues

16th—Fort Fisher has fallen; Wilmington will of course follow. This was our last port into which blockade-runners were successful in entering, and which furnished us with an immense amount of store. What will be the effect of this disaster we know not; we can only hope and pray.

Constance Cary Harrison's Recollections Continue

The engagement of my cousin Hetty Cary to Brigadier-General John Pegram having been announced, their decision to be married on January 19 was a subject of active interest . . . On the evening of January 19 all our little world flocked to St. Paul's Church to see the nuptials of one called by many the most beautiful woman in the South, with a son of Richmond universally honored and beloved. [13]

Judith McGuire Diary Continues

February 8—I feel more and more anxious about Richmond. I can't believe that it will be given up; yet so many persons are doubtful that it makes me very unhappy. I can't keep a regular diary now, because I do not like to write all that I feel and hear. I am constantly expecting the blessing of God in a way that we know not. I believe that all of our difficulties are to be overruled for good. A croaker accuses me of expecting a miracle to be wrought in our favor, which I do not; but we have been so often led on in a manner so wonderful that we have no right to doubt the mercy of God towards us. Our troops, too, are standing up under such hardships and trials, which require the most sublime moral as well as personal courage to endure, that I cannot avoid expecting a blessing upon them! . . .

28th—Our new Commissary-General is giving us brighter hopes for Richmond by his energy. Not a stone is left unturned to collect all the provisions from the country. Ministers of the Gospel and others have gone out to the various county towns and court-houses to urge the people to send in every extra bushel of corn or pound of meat for the army. The people only want enlightening on the subject; it is no want of patriotism which makes them keep any portion of their provisions. Circulars are sent out to the various civil and military officers in all disenthralled counties in the State,—to ask for their superfluities. All will answer promptly, I know, and generously. . . .

March 10—Still we go on as heretofore, hoping and praying that Richmond may be safe. Before Mr. H. left Richmond, I watched his countenance whenever I heard the subject mentioned before him, and though he said nothing, I thought he looked sad. I know that he understands the situation of affairs perfectly, and I may have fancied the sad look, but I think not; and whenever it arises before my mind's eye, it makes me unhappy. I imagine, too, from a conversation which I had with Mr. Secretary Mallory that he fears much for Richmond. Though it was an unexpressed opinion, yet I fear that I understand it rightly. I know that we ought to feel that whatever General Lee and the President deem right for the cause must be right, and that we should be satisfied that all will be well; but it would almost break my heart to see this dear old city, with its hallowed associations, given over to the federals. Fearful orders have been given in the offices to keep the papers packed, except such as we are working on. The packed boxes remain in the front room, as if uncertainty still existed about moving them. As we walk in every morning, all eyes are turned to the boxes to see if any have been removed, and we breathe more freely when we find them still there. . . .

11th—Sheridan's raid through the country is perfectly awful, and he has joined Grant, without being caught. Oh, how we listened to hear that he had been arrested in his direful career! I suppose, the most cruel and desolating raid upon record—more lawless, if possible, than Hunter's. He had an overwhelming force, spreading ruin through the Upper Valley, the Piedmont country, the tide-water country, until he reached Grant. His soldiers were allowed to commit any cruelty on non-combatants that suited their rapacious tempers—stealing everything they could find; ear-rings, breastpins, and finger-rings were taken from the first ladies of the land; nothing escaped them which was worth carrying off from the already desolated country. And can we feel patient at the idea of such soldiers coming to Richmond, the target at which their whole nations, from their President to the meanest soldier upon their army-rolls, has been aiming for four years. Oh, I would that I could see Richmond burnt to the ground by its own people, with not one brick left upon another, before its defenseless inhabitants should be subjected to such degradation!

Fighting is still going on; so near the city, that the sound of cannon is everywhere in our ears. Farmers are sending in produce which they cannot spare but which they give with a spirit of self-denial rarely equaled. Ladies are offering their jewelry, their plates, anything which can be converted into money for the country. I have heard some of them declare that, if necessary, they will cut off their long suits of hair and send them to Paris to be sold for bread for the soldiers; and there is not a woman, worthy of the name of Southerner, who would not do it, if we could get it out of the country, and receive bread or meat in return. Some gentlemen have given up their watches, when everything else has been given. A colonel of our army was seen the other night, after a stirring appeal had been made for food for the soldiers, to approach the speaker's stand with his watch in his hand, saying: "I have no money, nor provisions; my property was ruined by Hunter's raid last summer; my watch is very dear to me from association but it must be sold for bread." Remembering, as he put it down, that it had been long worn by his wife, now dead; though not a man who liked or approved of scenes, he obeyed the affectionate impulse of his heart, took it up quickly, kissed it, and replaced it on the table.

12th A deep gloom has just been thrown over the city by the untimely death of one of its own heroic sons. General John Pegram fell while nobly leading his brigade against the enemy in the neighborhood of Petersburg. . . .

Constance Cary Harrison's Recollections Continue

Three weeks later, to the day, General Pegram's coffin, crossed with a victor's palms beside his soldier's accoutrements, occupied the spot in the chancel where he had stood to be married. Besides it knelt his widow swathed in crape. Again Dr. Minnegerode conducted the ceremony, again the church was full. Behind the hearse, waiting outside, stood his war charger, with boots in stirrups. The wailing of the band that went with us on the slow pilgrimage to Hollywood will never die out of memory.

The newly married couple had gone directly to General Pegram's head-quarters, near Petersburg, where he was at the head of Early's division. Their new home was in a pleasant farm-house nine miles out of Petersburg, close to the line of General Pegram's command, near Hatcher's Run. Here, within constant sound of shot and shell, her taste and skill busied itself in fitting up rooms that seemed to her soldier the perfection of beauty and comfort, and in preparing for him little dishes that transformed their ordinary fare.

The ladies were at this time sitting in an ambulance at some distance away carding lint. At sunset a new charge was formed against the enemy,

General Pegram leading it, sword in hand, when a minie-ball (claimed to have been fired by a sharp-shooter a great way off) entered his heart, killing him instantly, after striking the sword from his hand and filling its scabbard with his blood.[14]

Judith McGuire's Diary Continues

31st—A long pause in my diary. Everything seems so dark and uncertain that I have no heart for keeping records. The croakers croak about Richmond being evacuated, but I can't and won't believe it.

There is hard fighting about Petersburg, and General A. P. Hill has been killed. Dreadful to think of losing such a man at such a time; but yet it comes nearer to home when we hear of the young soldiers whom we have loved, and whose youth we have watched with anxiety and hope as those on whom our country must depend in days to come, being cut down when their country most needs them. . . .

A week ago we made a furious attack upon the enemy's fortifications near Petersburg, and several were taken before daylight, but we could not hold them again overwhelming numbers, and batteries vastly too strong for any thing we could command, and so it is still—the enemy is far too strong in numbers and military resources. The Lord saves us, or we perish! Many persons think that Richmond is in the greatest possible danger, and may be evacuated at any time. Perhaps we are apathetic or too hopeful, but none of us are desponding at all, and I find myself planning for the future, and feeling excessively annoyed when I find persons less sanguine than myself.

CHAPTER SEVEN
April, 1865—Richmond Falls

"Alas! Every sight and sound was grievous and heavy."—Judith McGuire

Phoebe Yates Pember's Remembrances Continue

Early that fateful morning, Mayor Mayo, Judge Meredith and Judge Lyons went out to meet the incoming foe and deliver up the keys to the city. Their coach of state was a dilapidated equipage, the horses being raw-boned shadows of better days when there were corn and oats in the land. They carried a piece of wallpaper, on the unflowered side of which articles of surrender were inscribed in dignified terms setting forth that "It is proper to formally surrender the City of Richmond, hitherto the Capital of the Confederate States of America. [15]

Judith McGuire's Diary Continues

April 3—Agitated and nervous I turn to my diary to-night as the means to sooth my feelings. We have passed through a fatal thirty-six hours. Yesterday morning (it seems a week ago) we went, as usual, to St. James's Church, hoping for a day of peace and quietness, as well as of religious improvement and enjoyment. How short-sighted we are, and how little do we know of what is coming, either of judgment or mercy. The sermon being over, as it was the first Sunday in the month, the sacrament of the Lord's Supper was administered. The day was bright, beautiful, and peaceful, and a general quietness and repose seemed to rest upon the congregation, undisturbed by rumors and apprehensions. While the sacred elements were being administered, the sexton came in with a note to General Cooper, which was handed him as he walked from the chancel, and he immediately left the church. It made me anxious; but such things are not uncommon, and caused no excitement in the congregation. The services being over, we left the church, and as the congregations from the various churches were mingled on Grace Street. Our children, who had been at St Paul's, joined us, on their way to the usual family gatherings in our room on Sunday. After the salutations of the morning, J. remarked, in an agitated voice, to his father, that he had just returned from the war department, and that there was sad news—General Lee's lines had been broken, and the city would probably be evacuated within twenty-four hours. Not until then did I observe that every countenance was wild with excitement. The inquiry, "What is the matter?", ran from lip to lip. Nobody seemed to hear or to answer. An old friend ran across the street, pale with excitement, repeating what J. had just told us, that, unless we heard better news from General Lee, the city would be evacuated. We could do nothing; no one suggested any thing to be done. We reached home with a strange, unrealizing feeling. In an hour, J. received orders to accompany Captain Parker to the south with the Corps of Midshipmen. Then we began to understand that the Government was moving, and that the evacuation was indeed going on.

The office-holders were now making arrangements to get off. Every car was ordered to be ready to take to the south. Baggage-wagons, carts, drays, and ambulances were driving about the streets; every one was going off that could go, and now there were all the indications of alarm and excitement of every kind which attend such an awful scene. The people were rushing up and down the street; vehicles of all kinds were flying along, bearing goods of all sorts and people of all ages and classes who could go beyond the corporation lines. We tried to keep ourselves quiet. We could not go south, nor could we leave the city at all in this hurried way. J. and his wife had gone. The "Colonel", with B., intended going in the northern train this morning—he to his home in Hanover County, and she to her father's house in Clarke County, as soon as she could get there. Last night, when we went out to hire a servant to go to Camp Jackson for our sister, we for the first time realized that our money was worthless here, and that we are in fact penniless. About midnight she walked in, escorted by two convalescent soldiers. Poor fellows! We collected in one room, and tried to comfort one another; we made large pockets and filled them with as many of our valuables as we could suspend from our waists. The gentlemen walked down to the War Office in the night to see what was going on. Alas! Every sight and sound was grievous and heavy.

Phoebe Yates Pember's Remembrances Continue

My mind had been very unsettled as to my course of action in view of the impending crash, but my duty prompted me to remain with my sick, on the ground that no General ever desserts his troops. But to be left by all my friends to meet the dangers and privations of an invested city, among antagonistic influences, with the prospect of being turned out of my office the next day after the surrender was not a cheering one. Even my home would no longer be open to me; for staying with a cabinet minister, he would leave with the government.[16]

The officials of the various departments hurried to their offices, speedily packing up everything connected with the government. . . . Delicate women tottered under the weight of hams, bags of coffee, flour and sugar. Invalided officers carried away articles of unaccustomed luxury for sick wives and children at home. Every vehicle was in requisition, commanding fabulous remuneration, and gold and silver the only currency accepted. The immense concourse of government employees, speculators, gamblers, strangers, pleasure and profit lovers of all kinds that had been attached to that great center, the Capital, were 'packing" while those who had determined to stay and await the chances of war, tried to look calmly on, and draw courage from their faith in the justness of their cause. . . . Hour after hour fled and still the work went on. The streets were strewn with torn papers, records and documents too burdensome to carry away, too important to be left for inspection, and people still thronged the thoroughfares, loaded with stores until then hoarded by the government and sutler shops.[17]

Sallie Brock Putnam's Recollections Continue

The direful tidings spread with the swiftness of electricity. From lip to lip, from men, women, children, and servants, the news was bandied, but many received it at first, as only a "Sunday sensation rumor." Friend looked into the face of a friend to meet only an expression of incredulity; but later in the day, as the truth, stark and appalling, confronted us, the answering look was that of stony, calm despair. Late in the afternoon the signs of evacuation became obvious to even the most incredulous. Wagons were driven furiously through the street, to the different departments, where they received as freight, the archives of the government, and carried them to the Danville Depot, to be there conveyed by waiting by railroad cars.

Thousand of the citizens determined to evacuate the city with the government. Vehicles commanded any price in any currency possessed by the individual desiring to escape from the doomed capital. The streets were filled with excited crowds hurrying to the different transportation, intermingled with porters carrying huge loads, and wagons piled up with incongruous heaps of baggage, of all sorts and descriptions. The banks were all open, and depositors were busily and anxiously collecting the specie deposits and directors were as busily engaged in getting off their bullion. Millions of dollars of paper money, both state and Confederate, were carried to the Capital Square and buried.

Night came on, but with it no spell for human eyes in Richmond. Confusion reigned, and grim terror spread in wild contagion. The City Council met, and ordered the destruction of all spirituous liquors, fearing lest, in the excitement, there would be temptation to drink and render our situation still more terrible. In the gutters ran a stream of whiskey, and its fumes filled and impregnated the air. After night-fall, Richmond was ruled by the mob. In the principal business section of the city, they surged in one black mass from store to store, breaking them open, robbing them, and in some instances (it is said) applying the torch to them.

In the alarm and terror, the guards of the State Penitentiary fled from their posts, and the numbers of the lawless and desperate villains incarcerated there, for crimes of every grade and hue, after setting fire to their workshops, made good the opportunity for escape and donning garments stolen where they could get them, in exchange for their prison livery, roamed over the city like fierce, ferocious beasts. No human tongue, no pen, however gifted, can give an adequate description of the events of that awful night.

While these fearful scenes were being enacted on the streets, in-doors there were scarcely less excitement and confusion; into every house terror penetrated. Ladies were busily engaged in collecting and secreting all the valuables possessed by them, together with cherished correspondence; yet they found time and presence of mind to prepare a few comforts for friends forced to depart with the army or the government. Few tears were shed; there was no time for weakness or sentiment. The grief was too deep, the agony too terrible to vent through ordinary channels of distress. Fathers, husbands, brothers and friends clasped their loved ones to their bosoms in convulsive and agonized embraces, and bade an adieu, oh, heart-rendering-perhaps, thought many of them, forever. [18]

Fannie Taylor Dickinson's Letter

April 4, 1865—O happy days now gone by. I fear never to return; How my thoughts go back now to times which I then did not half appreciate, when I was often unhappy and ungrateful, sighing for better things, and yet compared to the present, every hour, every moment was one of joy. Then whatever other trouble was ours we had the feeling that our beloved city was still spared from our terrible foe. Then our streets were undesecrated by the tramp of their feet marching among us, treading out liberty and joy from every loyal heart. And now what a change! I cannot realize the dread fact that the hated enemy is here in our midst surrounding our homes, and daily, hourly are we to meet them, and perhaps talk with them and hear their taunts while we must be silent lest an unguarded word should draw upon us ill treatment. My thoughts seem in a perfect tumult, yet how to keep them down when I think of our brave soldiers and the blood of thousands of these precious ones which has been shed for the deliverance of our city, and yet, now, all in vain. Yet I would thank God that we have been spared so long; our mercies as a family and individuals have indeed been great. We have all been spared, and though now separated from all our brothers, yet I would trust and pray we will meet again.

We all went as usual to church. Dr. Jeter spoke with unusual earnestness, at the close referring with much feeling to the fact that he might soon be denied the liberty of speaking to us. How shortsighted we are, for as he spoke I thought it was impossible we should soon, if ever be under Yankee rule. We came home and ate our dinner in peaceful quiet. About an hour after dinner my sister came in asking, "Have you heard the news? Mr. Ritter says the Yankees will be here tomorrow. And Richmond will be evacuated!"

I felt appalled, yet could not half believe it true. We had so often heard such dismal tidings and later found it to be false. But the tears would come as I thought it might indeed be true. Presently a note was brought up from Cousin Cornelia, and as I read it each sentence seemed to burn itself into my brain—"A telegram from Lee, his lines broken in three places, Richmond must be given up, etc." My head sank and I gave way to scalding floods of sobs and tears, going into another room in order that the little children might not be alarmed. Soon felt that I must go down and be with the family to hear and talk and mingle tears together. How we bemoaned our fate, formed plans, and could hardly finish each sentence, hoping we might yet be able to hold our beloved city. After company left, we commenced the work of hiding. Sis Jane and Mother, with their accustomed celerity and energy, were disposing many pieces of bacon in safe places. While resting from the work Mr. S. came in, right from Petersburg, not knowing what to do or where to go, yet hardly believing matters were as far gone as we had heard.

O what a night that was to us! Knowing that Charlie must leave before light, having been told by General Ewell that it would not be safe to be here after daybreak, we determined not to go to bed. The others sat up all night. I, feeling perfectly exhausted, lay down with my clothes on for an hour or two, but not to sleep, my system seemed to have received a shock. Mother and Sis Jane did some necessary sewing for Charlie.

About one o'clock, Mr. D. and Mr. H. came up on horseback. They described the confusion and excitement down town as being great: bonfires burning, whiskey poured out on the street, cannons and wagons in motion. The two men still could not comprehend the true state of things until they reached home and heard our account. Mr. D. seemed perfectly stunned, I think he hardly knew what he said or did. He first thought of sending his servants off with Charlie, then thinking it would probably be a useless endeavor, gave it up.

In thankfulness yet sorrow, we ate our breakfast and assembled for family worship. Oh, what a prayer Mr. D. offered, so tender, so submissive—I hope I shall never forget it. Afterwards we continued our work of concealment while every few moments our ears were saluted by constant explosions. Presently we heard the sound of cheering and the drum and fife and, going to the upper windows, behold—oh, humiliating sight—a Yankee crowd marching up Broad Street with the stars and stripes floating. They entered the field just opposite our home and seemed to be coming right across. They planted the flag about halfway and there they stationed themselves. Mr. D. and Mr. H., feeling the necessity of our being protected, went over to secure a guard. He soon returned, having conversed with two officers who assured us we would not be molested. This was about half past ten o'clock. Just then the cars came in from Ashland and, as we had fondly hoped, Father in them. Presently he came in and was so much affected, he could hardly speak. Then we all sat down and talked as calmly as we could. [19]

Letter from Mrs. A. Fontaine to Marie Burrows Sayre, Richmond, Va.

. . . Presently there were rumors that General Lee's line was broken, and the enemy had reached the railroad, and Richmond must fall, etc. etc. We ladies were not contented except in the yard, and all were in the street with troubled faces. Major Williamson came to prepare a letter; then, one by one, the gentlemen hurried up with orders to leave that night. Then Mr. Davis, oh, so bowed and anxious came, and he told us that he feared Richmond must be evacuated by midnight, the truth was forced upon us. We turned to our rooms to prepare those who were to leave. Mrs. Williamson gave herself to grief which was terrible. All through that long, long night we worked and wept and bade farewells, never thinking of sleep; in the distance we heard shoots of the soldiers and mob as they ransacked stores; the rumbling of wagons, and beating of drums. all mixed in a confused medley. Just before dawn explosions of gun boats and magazines shook the city, and glass was shattered, new houses crumbled beneath the shocks. Involuntarily, I closed the shutters, and then everything had become still as death, while immense fires stretched their arms high around me. I shuttered at the dreadful silence. Richmond burning and no alarm. It was terrible! I cannot describe my feelings as I stood at a window overlooking the city in that dim dawn. I watched those silent, awful fires. I felt that there was no effort to stop them, but all like myself were watching them, paralyzed and breathless. After a while the sun rose as you may have seen it, a great red ball veiled in a mist. Again the streets were alive with hurrying men and women, and the cry of "Yankees" reached me. I did not move. I could not, but watched the blue horsemen ride to City Hall, enter, with his swords knocking the ground at every step, and threw the great doors open, and take possession of our beautiful city; I watched two blue figures on the Capitol, white men, I saw them unfurl a ting flag, and then I sank on my knees, and the bitter, bitter tears came in a torrent. [20]

. . . About eight o'clock, after some 30 Cavalry men had taken possession of Richmond, hoisted their flag, etc., the Artillery came dashing up Broad Street, positively the fattest horses came trotting up that heavy hill, dragging the cannon as though they were light carriages, the trappings were gay, and I commenced to realize the fearful odds against which our gallant little army had contended. Then the infantry came playing "The Girl I left behind" that dear old air that we heard our brave men so often play; then the negro troops playing "Dixie". . . . Then our Richmond servants were completely crazed, they danced and shouted, men hugged each other, and women kissed, and such a scene of confusion you have never seen. Imagine the streets crowded with these wild people, and troops by the thousands, some loaded with plunder from the burning stores, whole rolls of cloth, bags of corn, etc. chairs, one old women rolling a great sofa; dozens of bands trying to drown each other it seemed; gorgeously dressed officers galloping furiously about; men shouting and swearing as I have never hear men do it before; the fire creeping steadily neared to us, until houses next to us caught, and we prepared to leave; and above all, inconceivably terrible, the 700,000 shells exploding at the laboratory. I say imagine, but you cannot; no one who was not here will every fully appreciate the horrors of that day. Some say it was like their idea of the judgment day; perhaps it may be. So many shells exploding for five hours would be fearful at any time; the heavens were black as with a thunder cloud, great pieces of shells flying about; oh! It was too awful to remember . . . [21]

Letter from Constance Cary Harrison to her Mother and Brother dated April, 4 1865

. . . I ought to tell you the important news that your tin box of securities is safe and in my keeping. How do you think this happened? On Sunday, after Clarence left, and we were wandering around the streets like forlorn ghosts, I chanced to meet our friend, Mr.—, the president of the—Bank, in which I knew you kept them. He was very pale and wretched looking, said he could not vouch for the safe-keeping of anybody's property, asked after you and wondered if I would feel like taking your papers in charge. I walked with him to the bank where he put the box in my hands and then I hurried back with it to my uncle's house. I slept with the papers under my head Sunday night, and spent Monday afternoon in ripping apart the trimming of my gray beige skirt. You know that trimming, like a wide battlement of brown silk all around the hem? Well, into this wall of Troy I sewed with the tightest stitches I could make (You would say those were nothing to boast of, remembering the sleeve that came apart.) every one of your precious documents. And here I am with the family fortune stitched into my frock, which I have determined to wear every day with a change of white bodices, till I see you or can get to some place where it is safe to take it off. . . .

I will say in concluding the episode of the hidden papers, that the next day after I had received them, the bank went down in the track of the awful Main Street fire, its contents destroyed utterly. I continued to wear the skirt, heartily sick of it before I dared lay the thing aside, until the day in late April when I went by flag of truce to Baltimore, and there, at the home of my uncle, Mr. Cary, extracted the papers, put them in a new tin box, and consigned them to proper safe-keeping. I have certainly never since worn a gown of the value of that one, ungratefully cast aside at the first opportunity!

And what will you say when I tell you that my one and only book, like poor Mr. John R. Thompson's 'Across the Atlantic,' has gone up in flames and smoke, in the establishment of 'Messrs. West and Johnson, Publishers,' who lost everything in the fire? A little while ago, I should have wanted to cry over this calamity. So many pages of good Confederate fool's cap closely scribbled over; so much eloquence and pathos lost to the world forever! Really now, joking apart, if West and Johnson, who are clever men, hadn't thought it worth publishing they wouldn't have accepted it, would they? Now—now—nothing seems to hurt much, in the fall of our Confederacy. Perhaps my poor 'Skirmishing' has made more of a blaze in the world in this way, than it ever would have done in the ordinary course of events! [22]

Judith McGuire's Diary Continues

April 3 (Cont.)—A telegram just received from General Lee hastened the evacuation. The public was to be forsaken. They said that by three o'clock in the morning the work must be completed to make the city ready for the enemy to take possession. . . . Hope seemed to fade; none but despairing words were heard, except from a few Union men who began to show themselves; treason walked abroad. A gloomy pall came over us; but I do not think that any of us felt keenly, or have yet realized our calamity. The suddenness and extent of it is too great for us to feel its poignancy. Two o'clock in the morning we are startled by a loud sound like thunder the house windows rattled; it seems like an earthquake in our midst. We knew not what happened. It was soon understood to be the blowing up of a magazine. A few hours later another exploded on the outskirts of the city, much louder than the first. The Colonel and B. had just gone. Shall we ever leave? Many ladies were now upon the streets. The lower part of the city was burning. I set off to go to the central depot to see if the cars would go out. As I walked down Franklin to Broad Street, on Broad, the pavements were covered with broken glass. Women, both white and colored, were walking in multitudes from the Commissary with bags of flour, meal, coffee, sugar, rolls of cotton cloth, etc.; carts and rolling wheelbarrows filled in the same way. I went on and on and the shouts and screams became louder. The rabble rushed by me in one stream. At last I exclaimed, "Who are those shouting? What is the matter?" I seemed to be answered by a hundred voices, "The Yankees have come." I turned to come home, but what was my horror, when I reached Ninth Street, to see a regiment of Yankee cavalry come dashing up, yelling, shouting, hallooing, and screaming. All bedlam let loose could not have vied with them in diabolical roaring. I stood riveted on the spot; I could not move nor speak. Then I saw the iron gates of our time-honored and beautiful Capital Square, on the walks and greensward of which no hoof had been allowed to tread, thrown open and the cavalry dash in. I could see no more; I must go on with a mighty effort, or faint where I stood. I came home amid what I thought was the firing of cannon. I thought that they were thundering forth a salute that they had reached the goal of their ardent desires; but I afterwards found that the Armory was on fire, and that the flames having reached the shells deposited there for our army, they were exploding. Those explosions kept up until a late hour this evening; I am rejoiced they are gone; they, at least, can never be turned against us. I found the family collected around the breakfast-table, and we were glad to see Captain M's family with them. The Captain has gone, and the ladies have left their home on "Union Hill" to stay here among friends. Colonel P. having kindly given them rooms. An hour or two after breakfast we all retired to our rooms exhausted. No one had slept; no one had sought repose or thought of their own comfort. The federal soldiers were roaming about the streets; either whiskey or the excess of joy had given some of them the appearance of being beside themselves.

Phoebe Yates Pember's Remembrances Continue

Before three hours had elapsed, the troops had been quartered and were inspecting the city. They swarmed in every highway and byway, rose out of gullies, appeared on the top of hills, emerged from narrow lanes, and skirted around low fences. There was hardly a spot in Richmond not occupied by a blue coat but they were orderly, quiet and respectful. Thoroughly disciplined and warned not to give offence by look or act, they did not speak to any one unless first addressed; and though the women of the south contrasted with sickness of heart the difference between this splendidly-equipped army and the war-worn, wasted aspect of their own defenders, they were grateful for the consideration shown them; and if they remained in their sad homes, with closed doors and windows or walked the streets with averted eyes and veiled faces, it was that they could not bear the presence of invaders, even under the most favorable circumstances.

Before the day was over, the public buildings were occupied by the enemy, and the minds of the citizens relieved from fear of molestation. The hospitals were attended to, the ladies being allowed to nurse and care for their own wounded; but rations could not be drawn yet, the obstruction in the James River preventing the transports from coming up to the city. In a few days they arrived, and food was issued to those in need. [23]

Sallie Brock Putnam's Recollections Continue

As the sun rose on Richmond, such a spectacle was presented as can never be forgotten by those who witnessed it. To speed destruction, some malicious and foolish individual had cut the hose in the city. The fire was progressing with fearful rapidity. The roaring, the hissing, and the crackling of the flames were heard above the shouting and confusion of the immense crowd of plunderers who were moving amid the dense smoke like demons, pushing, rioting and swaying with their burdens to make passage to the open air. From the lower portion of the city, near the river, dense, black clouds of smoke arose as a pall of crape to hide the ravages of the devouring flames, which lifted their red tongues and leaped from building to building as if possessed of demonic instruct and intent on wholesale destruction.

By this time the flames had been applied to or had reached the arsenal, in which several hundred car loads of loaded shells were left. At every moment the terrific explosions were sending forth their awful reverberations, and gave us the idea of a general bombardment. All the horrors of the final conflagration, when the earth shall be wrapped in flames and melt with fervent heat, were, it seemed to us, prefigured in our capital.

As early as eight o'clock in the morning, while the mob held possession of Main Street, and were busily helping themselves to the contents of the dry goods stores and other shops in that portion of the city, and while a few of our old cavalry were still to be seen here and there in the upper portions, a cry was raised: The Yankees! The Yankees are coming!" Major A. H Stevens of the Fourth Massachusetts Cavalry, and Major E.E. Graves, of his staff, with forty Cavalry, rode steadily into the city, proceeding directly to the Capitol, and planted once more the "Stars and Stripes"—the ensign of our subjugation-on that ancient edifice. As its folds were giving out the breeze, while still we heard of the roaring, hissing, crackling flames, the explosions of the shells, and the shouting of the multitude, the strains of an old familiar tune floated upon the air—a tune that, in days gone by, was wont to awaken a thrill of patriotism. But now only the most bitter and crushing recollections awoke within us, as upon our quickened hearing fell the strains of "The Stars Spangled Banner." For us it was a requiem for buried hopes. . . .

By one o'clock the confusion reached its height. As soon as the Federal troops reached the city they were set to work by the officers to arrest the progress of the fire. By this time a winds had risen from the south, and seemed likely to carry the surging flames all over the northwestern portion of the city. The most strenuous efforts were made to prevent this, and the grateful thanks of the people of Richmond are due to General Weitzel and other officers for their energetic measures to save the city from entire destruction.

The Capital Square now presented a novel appearance. On the south, east and west of its lower half, it was bounded by burning buildings. The flames bursting from the windows, rising from the roofs, were proclaiming in one wild roar their work of destruction. . . . On the sward of the Square, fresh with the emerald green of early spring, thousands of wretched creatures, who had been driven from their dwellings by the devouring flames, were congregated. Fathers and mothers, weeping frightened children sought this open space for a breath of fresh air. But here, even, it was almost as hot as a furnace. . . . Along the north side of the Square were tethered the horses of the Federal cavalry, while, dotted about, were seen the white tents of the sutlers in which there were temptingly displayed canned fruits and meats, crackers, cheese, etc.

Above all these scenes of terror, hung a black shroud of smoke through which the sun shone with a lurid angry glare like an immense ball of blood that emitted sullen rays of light, as if loath to shine over a scene so appalling.

Remembering the unhappy fate of the citizens of Columbia and other cities of the South, and momentarily expecting pillage, and other evils incidental to the sacking of a city, great numbers of ladies sought the proper military authorities and were furnished with safeguards for the protection of themselves and their houses. These were willingly and generously furnished, and no scenes of violence are remembered too have been committed by the troops which occupied Richmond.

The sun had set upon this terrible day before the awful reverberations of exploding shells at the arsenal ceased to be heard over Richmond. The evening came on. A deathlike quiet pervaded the late heaving and tumultuous city, broken only by the murmuring waters of the river. Night drew her sable mantle over the mutilated remains of our beautiful capital, and we locked, and bolted, and barred our doors; but sleep had fled our eyelids. All night long we kept a fearful vigil, and listened with beating heart and quickened ears for the faintest sound that might indicate the development of other and more terrible phases of horror. But from all these we were mercifully and providentially spared.

Upon reaching the city, General Weitzel established his headquarters in the Hall of the State Capitol and immediately issued an order for the restoration of quiet, and intended to allay the fears and restore confidence and tranquility to the minds of the inhabitants.

The principle pillar that sustained the Confederate fabric had been overthrown, the chief corner-stone had been loosened and pushed from its place, and the crumbling of the entire edifice to a ruined and shapeless mass, seemed to be but a question of time. [24]

Mary Tucker Magill's Chronicles Continue

The Capital Square presented a strange, sad picture; the fire had consumed everything consumable around three sides of its lower area, and the old Capitol stood alone, as it were in the midst of an island against the shores of which the waves of ruin beat.

Upon the green grass of the square sat, lay, or stood hundreds upon hundreds of human beings of all ages, sexes, and ranks of life, in various attitudes of despondency. There were the homeless outcasts of the fire; and above them waved and flapped the United States flag, the token of their defeat and humiliation, and around them the negro soldiers and the negroes of the city exulted and shouted over the triumphs of the day. [25]

After some days the disbanded soldiers of the dead cause began to flock back to the city, with bowed heads and bleeding hearts. They told with eloquence which alone is the offspring of true feelings, of the last hour of the life of the Army of Northern Virginia; of the hardship of the march, when the expected rations failed to reach them, and how the soldiers were obliged to scatter in order to get food to save them from starvation; how they lived for days on raw corn and even roots, but still the thought of surrender was far from them; and how when the hour for meeting the enemy arrived, and they were rushing on to the conflict; suddenly the field seemed to be alive with white flags, and their old warrior General riding into their midst, the tears streaming down his cheeks, said: "I have done what I could for you; I can do no more". [26]

Constance Cary Harrison's Letter to her Mother and Brother dated April 4, 1865

Grace Street, Richmond, April 4, 1865.

My precious Mother and Brother:

. . . Hardly had I seemed to have dropped upon my bed that dreadful Sunday night—or morning rather—when I was wakened suddenly by four terrific explosions, one after the other, making the windows of my garret shake. It was the blowing up, by Admiral Semmes, by order of the Secretary of the Navy, of our gunboats on the James, the signal for an all-day carnival of thundering noise and flames. Soon the fire spread, shells in the burning arsenals began to explode, and a smoke arose that shrouded the whole town, shutting out every vestige of blue sky and April sunshine. Flakes of fire fell around us, glass was shattered, and chimneys fell, even so far as Grace Street from the scene.

By the middle of the day poor Aunt M.'s condition became so much worse in consequence of the excitement, the doctor said she positively could not stand any further sudden alarm. His one comfort is that you, his dear sister, are taking care of his wounded boy of whom his wife has been told nothing. It was suggested that some of us should go to headquarters and ask, as our neighbors were doing, for a guard for the house where an invalid lay so critically ill. Edith and I were the volunteers for service, and set out for the Capital Square, taking our courage in both hands. Looking down from the upper end of the square, we saw a huge wall of fire blocking out the horizon. In a few hours no trace was left of Main, Cary, and Canal

Streets, from 8th to 18th Streets, except tottering walls and smoldering ruins. The War Department was sending up jets of flame. Along the middle of the streets smoldered a long pile, like street-sweepings, of papers torn from the different departments' archives of our beloved Government, from which soldiers in blue were picking out letters and documents that caught their fancy. The Custom House was the sole building that defied the fire amongst those environing the Square. The marble Statesman on the Monument looked upon queer doings that day, inside the enclosure from which all green was soon scorched out, or trampled down by the hoofs of cavalry horses picketed at intervals about it. Mr. Read's Church, Mrs. Stanard's house, the Prestons' house, are all burned; luckily the Lee house and that side of Franklin stand uninjured. General Lee's house has a guard camped in the front yard.

We went on to the headquarters of the Yankee General in charge of Richmond, that day of doom, and I must say were treated with perfect courtesy and consideration. We saw many people we knew on the same errand as ourselves. We heard stately Mrs.—and the—'s were there to ask for food, as their families were starving. Thank God, we have not fallen to that! Certainly her face looked like a tragic mask carved out of stone.

A courteous young lieutenant, now General Peck, U. S. A., was sent to pilot us out of the confusion, and identify the house, over which a guard was immediately placed. Already the town wore the aspect of one in the Middle Ages smitten by pestilence. The streets filled with smoke and flying fire were empty of the respectable class of inhabitants, the doors and shutters of every house tight closed. [27]

Through all this strain of anguish ran like a gleam of gold the mad vain hope that Lee would yet make a stand somewhere—that Lee's dear soldiers would give us back our liberty. Dr. Minnerode has been allowed to continue his daily services and I never knew anything more painful and touching than that of this morning when the Litany was sobbed out by the whole congregation. [28]

Judith McGuire's Diary Continues

April 3rd (cont)—We had hoped that very little whiskey would be found in the city as, by order of the Mayor, casks were emptied yesterday evening in the streets, and it flowed like water through the gutters; but the rabble had managed to find it secreted in the burning shops, and bore it away in pitchers and buckets. It soon became evident that protection would be necessary for the residences, and at the request of Colonel P. I went to the Provost Marshal's office to ask for it. Mrs. P. was unfortunately in the country, and only ladies were allowed to apply for guards. Of course this was a very unpleasant duty, but I must undertake it. Mrs. D. agreed to accompany me, and we proceeded to the City Hall, which from my childhood I had regarded with respect and reverence, as the place where my father had for years held his courts, and in which our lawyers whose names stand among the highest in the Temple of Fame, for fifty years expounded the Constitution and the laws, which must now be trodden under foot. We reached it. After passing through crowds of Negro soldiers there, we found on the steps some of the elderly gentlemen of the city seeking admittance, which was denied them. I stopped to speak to Mr.—, in whose commission house I was two days ago, and saw him surrounded by all the stores which usually make up the establishment of such a merchant; it was now a mass of blackened ruins. He had come to ask for protection for his residence, but was not allowed to enter. We passed the sentinel, and an officer escorted us to the room in which we were to ask our country's foe to allow us to remain undisturbed in our own houses. Mrs. D.—leant on me tremblingly; she shrank from the humiliating duty. For my own part, though my heart beat loudly and my blood boiled, I never felt more high-spirited or lofty than at that moment. A large table was surrounded by officials, writing or talking to the ladies, who came on the same mission that brought us. I approached the officer who sat at the head of the table, and asked him politely if he was the Provost Marshal. "I am the Commandant, madam," was the respectful reply. "Then to whom am I to apply for protection for our residence?" "You need none, madam; our troops are perfectly disciplined, and dare not enter your premises." "I am sorry to be obliged to undeceive you, sir, but when I left home seven of your soldiers were in the yard of the residence opposite to us, and one had already been into our kitchen." He looked surprised, and said "There, madam, you are entitled to a guard. Captain, write a protection for the residence on the corner of First and Franklin

Streets, and give these ladies a guard." This was quickly done, and as I turned to go out, I saw standing near me our old friend, Mrs.—. Oh! How my heart sank when I looked into her calm, sad face, and remembered that she and her venerable and highly esteemed husband must ask leave to remain in peace in their home of many years. The next person who attracted my attention was the sweet young girl, S. W.; having no mother, she of course must go and ask that her father's beautiful mansion may be allowed to stand uninjured. Tears rolled down her cheeks as she pressed my hand in passing. Others were there; we did not speak, we could not; we sadly looked at each other and passed on. Mrs. D.—and myself came out, accompanied by our guard. The fire was progressing rapidly, and the crashing sound of falling timbers was distinctly heard. Dr. Read's church was blazing. Yankees, citizens, and Negroes were attempting to arrest the flames. The War department was falling in; burning papers were being wafted about the streets. The Commissary Department, with our desks and papers, was consumed already.

Warwick & Barkdale's mill was sending its flames to the sky. Cary and Main Streets seemed doomed throughout; Bank Street was beginning to burn, and now it had reached Franklin. At any moment it would have distracted me, but I had ceased to feel any thing. We brought our guard to Colonel P., who posted him; about three o'clock he came to tell me that the guard was drunk, and threatening to shoot the servants in the yard. Again I went to the City Hall to procure another. I approached the Commandant and told him why I came. He immediately ordered another guard, and a corporal to be sent for the arrest of the drunken man. The flames had decreased, but the business part of the city was in ruins. The second guard was soon posted, and the first carried off by the collar. Almost every house is guarded; and the streets are now (ten o'clock) perfectly quiet. The moon is shining brightly on our captivity. God guide and watch over us!

Fannie Taylor Dickinson's Letter

It seemed to me the day would never end, and it was so filled with strange events, strange sights and strange sounds. At our corner was stationed a Yankee guard who, as each Negro woman and child passed by, were stopped and shaken hands with most vigorously, taking the little ones into the lap and treating all to whiskey. T'was indeed a disgusting sight.

That night a lieutenant who had been applied to for a guard, came over bringing a private to spend the evening. I stayed but a few minutes in their company for my heart rebelled so against them and my blood boiled as I heard him talk about all shaking hands and living under the stars and stripes once more.

From sheer exhaustion I slept soundly all night, waking early to feel oh so heavy at heart, yet so thankful we had been thus far protected from insult and injury. A Negro guard marched before our doors, assisted in turn by the neighbors as watch; dear Father walking from nine until one o'clock. [29]

CHAPTER EIGHT

1865—Richmond Occupied

"It is very hard to help from dreading what may befall us."—Judith McGuire

Phoebe Yates Pember's Recollections Continue

It had been a matter of pride among the Southerners to boast that they had never seen a greenback, so the entrance of the Federal army had thus found them entirely unprepared with gold and silver currency. People, who had boxes of Confederate money and were wealthy the day previously, looked around in vain for wherewithal to buy a loaf of bread. Strange exchanges were made on the street of tea and coffee, flour and bacon.

Those who were fortunate in having a stock of household necessaries were generous in the extreme to their less wealthy neighbors, but the destitution was terrible. The sanitary commission shops were opened and commissioners appointed by the Federals to visit among the people and distribute orders to draw rations, but to affect this, after receiving tickets, required so many appeals to different officials, that decent people gave up the effort. Besides, the musty cornmeal and strong cod-fish were not appreciated by fastidious stomachs—few gently nurtured could relish such unfamiliar food.

But there was no assimilation between the invaders and the invaded. In the daily newspaper, a notice had appeared that the military bands would play in the beautiful capital grounds every afternoon, but when the appointed hour arrived, except the Federal officers, musicians and soldiers, not a white face was to be seen. The Negroes crowded every bench and path.

The next week another notice was issued that the colored population would not be admitted; and then the absence of everything and anything feminine was appalling. The third week still another notice appeared: "colored nurses were to be admitted with their white charges", and lo! each fortunate white baby received the cherished care of a dozen finely-dressed black ladies, the only drawback being that in two or three days the music ceased altogether, the entertainers feeling at last the ingratitude of the subjugated people.

Bravely-dressed Federal officers met their former old class-mates from college and military institutions and inquired after the relatives to whose houses they had ever been welcome in the days of yore, expressing a desire to "call and see them." while the vacant chairs, rendered vacant by federal bullets, stood by the hearth of the widow and bereaved mother. They could not be made to understand that their presence was painful.

There were few men in the city at this time; but the women of the south still fought their battle for them: fought it resentfully, calmly but silently! Clad in their mourning garments, overcome but hardly subdued, they sat within their desolate homes, or if compelled to leave that shelter, went on their errands to church or hospital with veiled faces and swift steps. By no sign or act did the possessors of their fair city know that they were even conscious of their presence. If they looked in their fair faces they saw not; they might have supposed themselves a phantom army. There was no stepping aside with affection to avoid the contact of dress, no feigned humility in giving the inside of the walk; they simply ignored their presence.

Two particular characteristics followed the army in possession—the circus and booths for the temporary accommodation of itinerant venders. The small speculators must have supposed that there were no means of cooking left in the city, from the quality of canned edibles they offered for sale. They inundated Richmond with pictorial canisters at exorbitant prices, which no one had money to buy. Whether the supply of greenbacks was scant, or the people were not disposed to trade with the newcomers, they had no customers.

In a few days, steamboats had made their way to the wharves, though the obstructions still defied the ironclads, and crowds of curious strangers thronged the pavements, while squads of male pleasure-seekers scoured the streets. Gayly-dressed women began to pour in also, with looped-in skirts, very large feet, and great preponderance of spectacles. The Richmond women sitting by desolated firesides were astonished by the arrival of former friends, sometimes people moving in the best classes of society, who had the bad taste to make a pleasure trip to the mourning city, calling upon heart-broken friends of happier days in all the finery of the newest New York fashions, and in some instances forgiving their entertainers the manifold sins of the last four years in formal and set terms. [30]

(ed: In order to receive government rations, whites had to take an oath to support the U. S. Constitution and its government and to accept the end of slavery. Most Richmonders in the late spring of 1865 accepted the reality of Confederate defeat and took the oath. The military took other reasonable steps to insure the overt loyalty of the city's whites. General Halleck forbade display of the Confederate flag. The grey uniform could not be worn unless the insignia were covered or removed.)

Sallie Brock Putnam's Recollections Continue

A tissue of unhappy events had thrown the people of Richmond into the most painful and positive destitution. We have before mentioned the universal circulation of Confederate money. We have noticed the scarcity of provisions and the usual manner of living. The evacuation of the city found great numbers of the inhabitants totally without food, and entirely destitute of means by which it might be procured. The distress was wide spread, and to prevent the horrors of starvation immediate relief was demanded. In a very few days liberal assistance were extended through the Relief Association of the United States and the Christian Commission of the Federal Army, and the United States Sanitary Commission dispensed suitable delicacies, and what, indeed, in many instances, seemed luxuries to the sick and enfeebled.

To give an adequate idea of the extent of destitution, we notice, from the Richmond Whig, that Mr. J. L. Apperson, Secretary of the Relief Committee, reported that from the 8th to the 15th of April, inclusive, 17,367 tickets were issued, calling for 86,555 rations. When the number of inhabitants in the city of Richmond is taken into account, it will be seen that at least one-third of the entire population remaining in the city (and thousands had fled when it was surrounded) were driven to the humiliation of subsisting alone on supplies of food furnished them by the conquerors. The supplies consisted of the coarsest and most substantial quality of edibles, yet they were not ungratefully, though with sickened hearts, received by the miserable people who depended upon them to prevent hunger or starvation.

The miseries of our situation, which would have been incalculable at best, were inconceivably enhanced by the disastrous burning of the business portion of the city. Barely all the supplies of food were kept in the stores which were consumed by the fire, and our poor people were almost totally dependent upon the mercy of the captors. For several months no remunerative employment could be obtained by the masses, and they were compelled to live by charity. The humiliation of many of this means of livelihood cannot be estimated. Commissary stores, where rations were dispensed, presented a novel aspect. Intermingled in a strange, incongruous way, hitherto refined and delicately-nurtured of the women of Virginia were driven by cruel want to seek such substances with the coarse, rude and vulgar of questionable parts of the city, and, frequently with Negroes who had left their former homes, and who, thus, took their first step in freedom. [31]

(ed: The print on the cover of the book depicts this well.)

The occupation of Richmond by our enemies occurred at a peculiarly interesting period in the ecclesiastical division of the year. It was the last week of the Lenten season, the week which commemorates the passion of our Savior.

In the diocese of Virginia, the clause in the prayer for the "President of the United States, and all others in authority," had been altered by order of the Bishops, to correspond to our status under the Confederacy. The Bishop, being absent, it could not then be conveniently changed, and owing, as they felt they then owed, political allegiance only to the President of the Confederate States, and with no instruction at that time from their diocesan, to make use of the prayer differently, the protestant Episcopal ministers of Richmond could not conscientiously use the unamended prayer of the Prayer-book. They were therefore required by the military authorities of the city to close their churches. It was the mostly rigorous and aggravating feature of our peculiar situation, and was to be a direct blow upon the very root of the tree of religious liberty. In a few weeks thee unhappy disagreements were reconciled, and the Bishop directed the use of the unamended prayer in the churches.

There would be a failure in simple justice, and a compromise of conscientious generosity. Did we refuse to accord to those placed in temporary authority over us as military rulers of Richmond, the offering of sincere gratitude, for the respect, the kindness, the lenity with which the citizens were treated? For a conquered people, the lines had fallen to us in pleasant places. The names of Ord, Weitzel, Patrick, Dent, Manning, Mulford and others, cannot be remembered with unkindness. They softened greatly the first bitter experiences of our subjugation.

The vast armies of our conquerors, on their homeward march, now begin to pour through the streets of Richmond. Day after day, as we witnessed the passage of the countless, and as they seemed to us interminable legions of the enemy, against which our comparatively little army had so obstinately, and all but successfully held out for four years; the questions that arose in our minds, was not why we were conquered at last, but "how we could have so long resisted the mighty appliances which operated against us." Our pride, our glory in our countrymen was heightened, and we felt indeed, "the South is the land for soldiers," and, though our enemies triumphed, it was at a price that we felt by them. [32]

Fannie Taylor Dickinson' Diary Continues

Tuesday morning (4/4). The Yankee captain with whom Mr. D. conversed came to breakfast. He seemed to be a gentlemanly man but I cannot enjoy or hardly tolerate his company. Little Jimmie, good rebel that he is, was really angry when he heard that a Yankee would sit at the table with us, and said, "I shan't stay at the table if that bad Yankee is coming." and cast many looks of defiance at him as he sat opposite. I feel that whenever I am with any of them, it would do me good to express just what I feel, but of course, prudence says, "Keep silent." . . .

About ten o'clock Mary answered a knock at the door and presently came in half leading, half supporting, Mary Harris. She was weeping and came throwing her arms around me, saying, "My husband is dead." I did not know her at first, but Mary told me; poor thing, how much she has gone through. Her husband died Monday. She thought his death was caused by the exciting news of the Yankee approach. She had walked all the way from Chimborazo Hospital with her child and nurse, about four miles, through crowds of soldiers, Negroes and women of all sorts, talking and shouting, elbowing her so that she could scarcely get along. On going to where she expected to find a house of a friend, only smoking ruins met her eyes. . . .

Wednesday morning. (4/5) Another long day. It is a humiliating thought that so many who have until now, declared for the South, should now proclaim themselves Union, and boldly tell our triumphant foe they have always been so. How my blood boiled as I heard such sentiments from Mr. and Mrs. H. who have lost a son in the army. I feel that it was doing a cruel wrong to his memory in saying that I was opposed to the cause for which he bravely fought and shed his blood. . . . It seems strange to have a guard always walking up and down before our front gate, and another in our stable lot. I feel as a prisoner in our own house. And so we are to all intents and purposes, for we cannot take any pleasure or feel at ease in walking out now. [33]

Judith McGuire's Diary Continues

April 5—I feel as if we were groping in the dark; no one knows what to do. The Yankees, so far, have behaved humanely. As usual, they begin with professions of kindness to those whom they have ruined without justifiable cause, without reasonable motive, without right to be here, or anywhere else within the Southern boundary. General Ord is said to be polite and gentlemanly, and seems to do every thing in his power to lessen the horrors of this dire Ord calamity. Other officers are kind in their departments, and the Negro regiments look quite subdued. No one can tell how long this will last. Norfolk had its day of grace, and even New Orleans was not down-trodden at once. There are already apprehensions of evil. Is the Church to pray for the Northern President? How is it possible, except as we pray for all other sinners? But I pause for further development.

6ᵗʰ—Mr. Lincoln has visited our devoted city to-day. His reception was any thing but complimentary. Our people were in nothing rude or disrespectful; they only kept themselves away from a scene so painful. There are very few Unionists of the least respectability here; they met him (He was attended by Stanton and others.) with cringing loyalty, I hear, but the rest of the dismal collection were of the low, lower, lowest of creation. They drove through several streets, but the greeting was so feeble from the motley crew of vulgar men and women, that the Federal officers themselves, I suppose, were ashamed of it, for they very soon escaped from their disgraceful association. It is said that they took a collection at General Ord's, our President's house!! Ah! It is such a bitter pill. It would be better that the dear old house, with all its associations, so sacred to the Southerners, so sweet to us as a family, had shared in the general conflagration. Then its history would have been unsullied, though sad. Oh, how gladly would I have seen it burn! I have been nowhere since Monday, except to see my dear old friend Mrs. R., and to the hospital. There I am not much subjected to the harrowing of sights and sounds by which we are surrounded. The wounded must be nursed; poor fellows, they are so sorrowful! Our poor old Irishman died on Sunday. The son of a very old acquaintance was brought to our hospital a few days ago, most severely wounded—Colonel Charles Richardson, of the artillery. We feared at first that he must die, but now there is a little more hope. It is so sad that after four years of bravery and devotion to the cause, he should be brought to his native city, for the defense of which he would have gladly given his life, dangerously if not mortally wounded, when its sad fate is just decided. I love to sit by his bedside and try to cheer him; his friends seem to vie with each other in kind attention to him.

We hear rumors of battles, and of victories gained by our troops, but we have no certain information beyond the city lines.

Fannie Taylor Dickinson' Diary Continues

Friday (4/7)—What a strange sight was presented to us yesterday morning. Mr. Harris arrived on foot at our gate, but was not permitted to enter by the guard! Mother and the baby went out to see him and the child knew him directly, going to his arms when lifted over the gate. A chair was handed him to sit in the street. After several applications, a corporal came over and gave permission for Mr. H. to enter.

Saturday (4/8)—What a contrast to last Saturday. Then all was quiet and peaceful; now surrounded on all sides by federals we are kept in almost a constant state of alarm. It is very hard to help from dreading what may befall us. By dint of much perseverance and effort, Father has succeeded in getting all passports to leave, so, after an early dinner Mr. D., Mr. H. with his wife and child left in the buggy, the gentlemen to ride and walk alternately. Last night, on ringing the bell for Millie, she was nowhere to be found. Judy called out that she was probably at the camp. She has not since made her appearance. This evening others from the camp have taken our front parlor, I do trust it may be for the best. I miss Mr. D. and shall earnestly look for his return. What if we shall be compelled to be separated on account of the dreadful oath which may soon be administered!

Sunday, April 9—Today has been outwardly beautiful and calm. It seemed rather strange to be starting to Sunday school after remaining so close at home all week. . . . Everything was very quiet; we met no federal soldiers all the way down. Very few assembled at Sunday school. I had only one scholar but filled up my class from other classes whose teachers were absent. When I went upstairs my indignation was aroused by seeing two Yankees in the choir (although I believe they went by invitation), but still more so when Dr. Jeter invited a Yankee preacher into the pulpit. I could not keep back the tears as I thought of the wrongs our people have suffered, now how indignities were heaped upon us, in ministers coming thus like wolves in sheep's' clothing to insult us in our affliction. Dr Jeter preached a very good sermon. [34]

Mary Tucker Magill Chronicles Continue

4/9—It was the Sunday after the evacuations; the suffering people had most of them gone forth as usual to the churches, some as a matter of habit, some from curiosity, and others with a desire to obtain comfort in the house of God which was denied them in their closets; but it cannot be denied that the most melancholy feature of the then present feeling in the South was a tendency to infidelity, or at least skepticism. They had so long clung with undoubting confidence to the help of God, founded on the righteousness of their cause, the mind could not at once recover; it was at sea in a storm without a rudder or sail, grasping for the help that did not come; and in the despair which ensued, doubt took possession of it, and a sullen distrust even of its Maker.

No army could have behaved better under the circumstances than did the United State army. They not only committed no depredations, but they kept aloof from the people, recognizing at once the bitterness of feeling which must have way. So in the churches they sat off by themselves, instead of mingling with them. Very little allusion was made from the pulpits to the condition of affairs; indeed it has been forbidden so far as prayer from the Confederacy was concerned; but no order could govern the nation's heart, and many an anguished application ascended to heaven from those alters for the little band of fugitives whose cause was even then beyond the reach of prayer. [35]

One old Baptist minister prayed: "O Lord, thou who seest our hearts, knowest what we so earnestly desire but dare not specify in word, Grant it, O Lord, grant it!" [36]

Judith McGuire's Dairy Continues

4/9—Another gloomy Sabbath-day and harrowing nights. We went to St. Paul's in the morning, and heard a very fine sermon from Dr. Minnerode—at least so said my companions. My attention, which is generally riveted by his sermons, wandered continually. I could not listen; I felt so strangely, as if in a vivid, horrible dream. Neither President was prayed for; in compliance with some arrangement with the Federal authority, the prayer was used as for all in authority! How fervently did we pray for our own President! Thank God, our silent prayers are free from Federal authority. "The oppressor keeps body bound, but knows not what a range the spirit takes." Last night, (it seems strange that we have lived to speak or write of it) between nine and ten o'clock, as some of the ladies of the house were collected in our room, we were startled by the rapid firing of cannon. At first we thought that there must be an attack upon our city; bright thoughts of the return of our army darted through my brain; but the firing was too regular. We began to think it must be a salute for some great event. We threw up the windows, and saw the flashes and smoke of cannon towards Camp Jackson. Some one counted one hundred guns. What could it be? We called to passers-by: "What do those guns mean?" Sad voices answered several times: "I do not know." At last one voice pertly, wickedly replied: "General Lee has surrendered, thank God!" Of course we did not believe him, though the very sound was a knell. Again we called out: "What is the matter?" A voice answered, as if from a broken heart: "They say the General Lee has surrendered." We cannot believe it, but my heart became dull and heavy, and every nerve and muscle of my frame seemed heavy too. I cannot even now shake it off. We passed the night, I cannot tell how—I know not how we live at all. At daybreak, the dreadful salute commenced again. Another hundred guns at twelve today. Another hundred—can it be so? No, we do not believe it, but how can we bear such a doubt? Where are all our dear ones, our beloved soldiers, and our noble chief tonight, while the rain falls pitilessly? Are they lying in the cold, hard ground, sleeping for sorrow? Or are they moving southward triumphantly, to join General Johnston, still able and willing—all, far more than willing to avenge their country's wrongs? God help us!—We must take refuse in unbelief.

Fannie Taylor Dickinson' Diary Continues

Monday April 10[th.] O sorrowful day, O day of sorrows! Today we hear that Lee, our brave General Lee, with his army has surrendered. It cannot be true, and yet we do not blame General Lee, such confidence we have in his bravery and plans.

Monday April 17 Today our servants left. Father offered them higher wages but they preferred to set up for themselves. This is indeed the unkindest cut of all. I cannot write about it. [37]

Myrta Lockett Avary's Recollections Continue

Among many similar incidents of the times is this, as related by a prominent physician: Others of our physicians and surgeons found friends in Federal ranks. To how many poor Boys in Blue, longing for home and kindred, had not they and our women ministered! The orders of the Confederate Government were that the sick and wounded of both armies should be treated alike. True, nobody had the best of far, for we had it not to give. We were without medicines; it was almost impossible to get morphia, quinine, and other remedies. . . . But the most cruel shortage was in food. Bitter words in Northern papers and by Northern speakers—after our defeat intensified, multiplied, and illustrated—about our treatment of prisoners exasperated us. "Will they never learn," we asked "that on such rations as we gave our prisoners, our men were fighting in the field?" We had not food for ourselves; the North blockaded us so we could not bring food from the outside, and refused to exchange prisoners with us. What could we do?" [38]

On that morning of the occupation, our women sat behind closed windows, unable to consider the new path stretching before them. The way seemed to end at a wall. Could they have looked over sand seen what lay ahead, they would have lost what little heart of hope they had; could vision have extended far enough, they might have won it back; they would have beheld some things unbelievable.

The federals filled Libby prison with Confederates, many of whom were paroled prisoners found in the city. Distressed women surrounded the prison, begging to know if loved ones were there; others plead to take food inside. Some called, while watching windows: "Let down your tin cup and I will put something in it." Other cried "Is my husband in there? O, William, answer me if you are!" "Is my son, Johnny, here?" "O, please somebody tell me if my boy is in the prison!" Miss Emily passed quietly through the crowd, her hospital reputation securing admission to the prison; she was able to render much relief to those with and to subdue the anxiety of those without.

Some tiny lads mounted guard on the steps opposite Military Headquarters, and being intensely "rebel" and having no means to express defiance to the invaders, made faces at the distinguished occupants of the establishment across the way. General Patrick, Provost-Marshal General, sent a courteously worded note to their father, calling his attention to these juvenile demonstrations. He explained that while he was not personally disturbed by the exhibition, members of his staff were, and the children might get into trouble. The proper guardians of the wee insurgents, acting upon this information, their first battery unlimited on their door-step, saw that the artillery was retired in good order, and peace and normal countenances reigned over the scene of the late engagement.

General Shepley, Military Governor by (General) Weitzel's appointment, repeated this in substance by adding: The soldiers of the command will abstain from any offensive or insulting words or gestures towards the citizens." With less tact and generosity, he proceeded: "The Armies of the Rebellion, having abandoned their efforts to enslave the people of Virginia, have endeavored to destroy by fire their Capital. . . . The first duty of the Army of the Union will be to save the city doomed to destruction by the Armies of the Rebellion." That fling at our devoted army would have served as a clarion call to us—had any been needed—to remember the absent. [39]

These were the men of the Union Army who saved Richmond: The First Brigade, Third Division (Deven's Division), Twenty-fourth Army Corps, Army of the James, Brevet-Brigadier-General Edward H. Ripley commanding. This brigade was composed of the Eleventh Connecticut, Thirteenth New Hampshire, Nineteenth Wisconsin, Eighty-first New York, Ninety-eighth New York, One Hundredth New York and Thirty-ninth New York, Convalescent detachment from the second and third division of Sheridan's reinforcements. [40]

Mary Tucker Magill's Chronicles Continues

In what had been apprehended as the greatest evil of all, proved to the end a blessing, as it brought an element into the storm of disorder and misrule which in some degree quelled it. So far from committing deeds of violence, the first act of the Federal force was an organized steady exertion to subdue the fire and restore order; and by night the flames began to succumb to their efforts, and the fire sank down exhausted, but glowing with a smoldering rage which only watched an opportunity break out again with renewed violence.

The destitution in the city was fearful; all of the lower part of it had been consumed, and with it such provisions as it contained. Numbers had escaped from their burning homes with only their lives, and the fact that the only money the mass of the people possessed was the Confederate currency, reduced all classes alike to absolute want.

After a day or two, the Federal commandant of the post, recognizing the necessity for taking some steps to remove this terrible destitution, appointed officers who went around to each house in the city and issued rations to all alike. Some idea may be gathered of the condition of things from the report of the Secretary of the Relief Committee, who from the 8th of April to the 15th issued eighty-six thousand five hundred and fifty-five rations! A terrible picture is thus represented as thousands had fled the city and at least one-third of the remaining population must have subsisted upon the rations issued by their captures. [41]

Judith McGuire's Dairy Continues

Tuesday Night (11th)—No light on our sorrow—still, gloomy, dark, and uncertain. I went to-day to the hospital, as was my duty. My dear friend S.T. cheers me, by being utterly incredulous about the reported surrender. As usual, she is cheerfully devoting her powers of mind and body to her hospital. For four years she never thought of her own comfort, when by sacrificing it she could alleviate a soldier's sorrow. Miss. E. D. who has shared with her every duty, every self-sacrificing effort in behalf of our sick and wounded soldiers, is now enduring the keenest pangs of sorrow from the untimely death of her father. On the day of the evacuation, while walking too near a burning house, he was struck by a piece of falling timber, and the blow soon closed his long life. Alas! The devoted daughter, who had done so much for the other wounded, could do nothing for the restoration of one so dear to her.

Wednesday Night (12th)—We have heard nothing new to-day confirming the report of the surrender, which is perhaps the reason my spirit tells a little more light. We must hope, though our prospects should be as dark as the sky of this stormy night. Our wounded are doing well—those who remain in our hospital and the convalescents have been ordered to "Camp Jackson." Indeed, all the patients were included in the same order; but Miss T. having represented that several of them were not in a condition to be removed, they have been allowed to remain where they are.

Mrs. M. E. Garthright's Writings to her Grandchildren

But, though Richmond had fallen, our glorious Lee, with 15,000 half-starved and three quarter clothed, men, still kept Grant at bay. Grant who stood at the head of what he declared to be the "finest army the world ever saw!"

But on the tenth the end came! We are only fifteen miles from Appomattox; and for days the dear soldiers, starved, ragged and foot-sore, were passing; getting to their southern homes as best they could with no money, only a few mounted on bags of bones, that had once been horses. They tell of a great many acts of kindness from the Yankees. Grant, himself, was a noble example by his generosity to our own dear Lee and to his officers.

The Yankees could not restrain their surprise, when they saw the army that for months had kept their hordes back.

The first knowledge we had of the "end" was on the morning of the 11th. Mother and I were sitting on the porch knitting, as always, when a soldier with his toes out, no crown in his hat, a Yankee fatigue jacket on, and the remains of home-spun trousers limped up. We jerked off our rings and breast-pins and popped them into the toes of the sock we were knitting. The soldier dropped onto the step and groaned "Lee has surrendered".

Up I jumped, in my impulsive fashion, and cried "Go away from here, that is a Yankee story, a Confederate would die before he'd say it!" But he soon convinced us of the awful fact, and introduced himself as Major—, nephew of a friend of my mother.

Soon others straggled along, and all the comfort we had was in feeding them with the little we had left, and patching them up as well as we could.

But we had no shoes for them, and Oh! The poor bleeding feet! I shall see them as long as I live, and know that the owners were uncrowned heroes. Randolph and Jack came on the 12th. Their shirts were bundles of rags and dirt, for they had not a change for months. Mary and I sacrificed our calico dresses, and all the family turned in and made them shirts. Meanwhile the boys had to stay in bed. Loud and many were the calls from their room "to hurry up with those shirts." As heartbroken as they were, a smile would come, when we saw these aforetime dandies, emerge in their gorgeous array. Their vests had long ago gone the way of all confederate vests, i.e. as trouser seats. Randolph had bright green vines meandering over front and collar; and Jack was glorious in red roses.

What will become of all the confederate money? Someone suggested that we paper our rooms with it. . . . [42]

Myrta Lockett Avary's Recollections Continue

For months after the surrender, Confederates were passing through the country to their homes, and hospitality was free to every ragged and footsore soldier; the poor best the larder of every mansion afforded was at the command of the grey-jacket. How diffidently proud men would ask for bread, their empty pockets shaming them! When any man turned them off with cold words, it was not well for his neighbors to know, for so, he was like to have no more respectable guests. The soldiers were good company bringing news from far and wide. Most were cheerful, glad they were going home, undaunted by long tramps ahead. The soldier was used to hard marches. Now that his course was set towards where loved ones watched for his coming, life had its rosy outlook that turned to gray for some who reached the spot where home had stood to find only a bank of ashes. Reports of country through which they came were often summed up: "White folks in the fields, Negros flocking to towns. Freedmen's Bureau offices everywhere thronged with blacks". [43]

Judith McGuire's Dairy Continues

Thursday Night (13th)—Fearful rumors are reaching us from sources which it is hard to doubt, that it is all too true, and that General Lee surrendered on Sunday last, the 9th of April. The news came to the enemy by telegram during the day and to us at night by the hoarse and pitiless voice of the cannon. We know, of course, that circumstances forced it upon our great commander and his gallant army. How all this happened—how Grant's hundreds of thousands overcame our little band, history, not I, must tell my children's children. It is enough for me to tell them that all the bravery and self-denial could do has been done. We do not yet give up all hope. General Johnston is in the field but there are thousands of enemy to his tens. The citizens are quiet. The calmness of despair is written on every countenance. Private sorrows are upon us. We *know* of but few casualties

Good Friday (14th)—As usual, I went to the hospital, and found Miss T. in much trouble. A preemptory order has been given by the Surgeon-General to remove all patients. In the opinion of our surgeon, to five of them it would be certain death. The ambulances were at the door. Miss T. and myself decided to go at once to the Medical Director and ask him, to recall the order. We were conducted to his office, and, for the first time, since the entrance of the Federal army, were impolitely treated. On two occasions we had been obliged to make application to officials, and had been received with great respect and consideration, and we believe it has been uniformly the case; and we were, therefore, very much surprised when a request which seemed to us so reasonable was at first refused most decidedly. We would not give up our application, as it seemed to be a matter of life and death; so we told him what our surgeon said, and that we hoped he would reconsider his order. He replied, that he should send a surgeon with the ambulances, and if in his judgment they could be removed, it should be done, without hesitation, as he was determined to break up the small hospitals *which you have all about town* (ours is the only small hospital in town,) and that he had ordered neither rations nor medicines to be issued to them. Miss T. told him nothing of the sort was necessary; she never asked nor received rations from the Federal Government; that she had now but five men under her care, and they were desperately wounded, and she would greatly prefer that the hospital should be considered in the light of a private establishment, which she could take care of without asking help. A change came over his countenance, but not his manner; he brusquely told us that he would "see about it." In an hour afterwards the surgeon and ambulance came but after what seemed to me rather pompous display of surgical examination and learned medical terms, addressed to the lady-nurses, he determined to leave our dear mangled soldiers to our care. One of them is in a dying condition; he cannot survive many hours.

We had no service in our churches to-day. An order came out in this morning's paper that the prayers for the President of the United States must be used. How could we do it? Mr.—went to the hospital by the request of Colonel Richardson, and had prayers in his room. Ambulances are constantly passing with horses in the finest possible condition—even finer than ours were in the beginning of the war. It seems to me in passing strange that, with all their advantages, we kept them at bay so long, and conquered them so often. Had one port been left open to us—only one, by which we might have received food and clothing Richmond would not now be in their hands; our men were starved into submission.

Sunday, April 16— . . . Each day we have hoped on, and encouraged each other to hope that General Lee had perhaps not really surrendered, and our affairs in not quite so bad a condition, but certain confirmation has at least arrived. General Lee himself entered Richmond yesterday with his staff. This week has been if anything, more sadden than last. . . .

Sunday Night—Strange rumors are afloat tonight. It is said, and believed, that Lincoln is dead, and Steward much injured. As I passed the house of a friend this evening, she raised the window and told me the report. Of course I treated it as a Sunday rumor; but the story is strengthened by the way which the Yankees treat it. They, of course, know all about it, and tomorrow's papers will reveal the particulars. I trust that, if true, it may not be by the hand of an assassin, though it would seem to fulfill the warnings of Scripture. His efforts to carry out his abolition theories has caused the shedding of oceans of Southern blood, and by man it now seems has his blood been shed. But what effect will it have on the South? We have much to fear. Future events will show. This event has made us wild with excitement and speculation

General Lee has returned. He came unattended, save by his staff—came without notice, and without parade; but he could not come unobserved; as soon as his approach was whispered, a crowd gathered in his path, not boisterously, but respectfully, and increasing rapidly as he advanced to his home on Franklin Street, between 8th and 9th, where, with a courtly bow to the multitude, he at once retired to the bosom of his beloved family. When I called in to see his high minded and patriotic wife, a day or two after the evacuation, she was busily engaged in her invalid's chair, and very cheerful and hopeful. "The end is not yet," she said, as if to cheer those around her, "Richmond is not the Confederacy." To this we all most willingly assented, and felt very much gratified and buoyed by her brightness. I have not had the heart to visit her since the surrender; but our hearts sink within us when we remember that he and his noble army are now idle, and that we can no longer look upon them as the bulwark of our land. He has returned from defeat and disaster with the universal and profound admiration of the world, having done all that skill and valor could accomplish. The scenes of at the surrender were noble and touching. General Grant's bearing was profoundly respectful; General Lee's as courtly and lofty as the purest chivalry could require. The terms, so honorable to all parties, being complied with to the letter, our arms were laid down with breaking hearts, and tears such as the stoutest warriors may shed. "Woe worth the day!"

Tuesday (18th)—Lincoln is dead and others of the Cabinet attacked. How tangled up everything now appears, but God can make it plain. "His love in times past forbids me to think. He will leave me at last in trouble to sink."

Tuesday Night—I try to dwell as little as possible on public events. I only feel that we have no country, no government, and no future. I cannot, like some others, look with hope on Johnston's army. He will do what he can; but, ah, what can he do? Our anxiety now is that our President and other public men may get off in safety. O God! Have mercy upon them and help them! For ourselves, like the rest of the refugees, we are striving to get from the city. The stereotyped question when we meet is "When and where are you going?" Our country relatives have been very kind. My brother offers us an asylum in his devastated home at W. While there we must look around for some other place, in which to build up a home for our declining years. Property we have none—all gone. Thank God, we have our faculties; the girls and myself, at least, have health. Mr.—bears up under our difficulties with the same hopeful spirit which he has ever manifested. "The Lord will provide," is still his answer to any doubt on our part. The Northern officials offer free tickets to persons returning to their homes—alas! To their homes! How few of us have homes! Some are confiscated; others destroyed. The families of the army and navy officers are here. The husbands and sons are absent, and they remain with nothing to anticipate and nothing to enjoy. Today I met a friend, the wife of a high official, whose hospitality I have often enjoyed in one of the most elegant residences in Virginia which has been confiscated and used as a hospital for "contrabands." Our conversation naturally turned on our prospects. Hearing where we are going, she replied, "I have no brother, but when I hear from my husband and son, I shall accept the whole-souled invitation of a relative in the country, who has invited me to make his house my home; but she added, as her beautiful eyes filled with tears "When are our visits to end? We can't live with our ruined relatives, and when our visits are over, what then? And how long must our visits of charity last?" The question was too sad; neither of us could command our voices, and we parted in silence and tears.

20th—The cars on the Central Railroad will run tomorrow, for the first time, under Federal rule, and the day after we will use our passports and free tickets to leave the city—dearer than ever, in its captivity and ruin. It is almost impossible to get current money. A whole-hearted friend from Alexandria met me the other day, and with the straightforward simplicity due to friendship in these trying times, asked me at once, "Has your husband any money?" I told him I thought not. He replied, "Tell him I have between twenty-five and thirty dollars—that's all—and he shall have half of it; tell him I say so." Ten dollars were accepted, for the circumstances of want which pressed so hard, and for the kindly spirit in which it was offered. Two other friends came forward to share with us their little all. God help the warm hearts of our conquered but precious country! I know that they will be blessed, and that light will yet shine through the blackness of darkness which now surrounds them.

W., 24th—On Saturday evening my brother's wagon met us at the depot and brought us to this place, beautiful in its ruins. We have not been here since the besom of destruction swept over it, and to us, who have been in the habit of enjoying its hospitality when all was bright and cheerful, the change is very depressing. We miss the respectful and respectable servants, born in the family and brought up with affection for the household which seemed a part of their nature, and which so largely contributed to the happiness both of master and servant. Even the nurse of our precious little J., the sole child of the house, whose heart seemed bound up in her happiness, is gone. It is touching to hear the sweet child's account of the shock she experienced when she found that her "mammy", deceived and misleads by the minions who followed Grant's army, had left her; and to see how her affection still clings to her, showing itself in the ardent hope that her "mammy" has found a comfortable home. The army had respected the interior of the house, because of the protection of the officers. Only one ornament was missing, and that was the likeness of this dear child. Since the fall of Richmond, a servant of the estate, who had been living in Washington, told me that it was in the possession of the maid-servant of the house, who showed it to him, saying that she "looked at it every day." We all try to be cheerful and to find a bright side; and we occupy time as cheerfully as we can. The governess having returned to her home in Norfolk, I shall employ myself in teaching my bright little niece here and the dear children at S. H. and feel blessed to have so pleasant a duty.

Emmie Sublett Letter to Emilie Anderson, Richmond, Virginia

Waverly Place, April 29, 1865

My darling Emilie-

. . . I never dreamed of the Yankees getting to Richmond sure enough, but the wretches are here. . . . O, the horrible wretches! I can't think of a name horrible enough to call them. It makes us fifty times more Southern in our feelings to have them here, though they have behaved very well indeed; no private property has been touched and no insults have been offered to any of the citizens. They say they can't get anything to report the Richmond girls for, to save their lives. They all behave with such perfect dignity and coolness, always go out thickly veiled and never notice the Yankees in the least. I've nearly broken my neck holding such a high head, ne'r condescending to look at one when I meet him. Our paroled prisoners are coming slowly in; poor fellows! They are all so sad. Gen. Lee is completely crushed; I never saw anything like it. I do feel so sorry for him. . . . The Yanks are very lenient to us at present, but they are drawing the ropes tighter and tighter every day. I believe there is some villainy at the bottom of it all. I am so sorry Lincoln was killed. I don't know what in the world to do, because I believe the whole South will be punished for it. Johnson will be such an awful President; he is a perfect old tyrant.

Emmie [44]

Letter from Mrs. A. Fontaine to Marie Burrows Sayre, Richmond, Va.

Richmond, Va. April 30th 1865

My Dear Cousin:

. . . We Richmond people have grown calm somewhat. The young ladies keep themselves quietly at home, doing nothing to expose themselves to insult; and in all cases declining controversy with the U. S. Officers, which I heartily approve. The question is closed for the present. And no lady ought to permit a discussion at all, because they have the advantage of success and the law, and it is not a fair contest. For my own part I tread my own path, utterly ignoring them. I do not seem to see them, careful only not to expose myself to insult. . . .

. . . We had a number of sudden marriages last Sunday. An order being issued Saturday, that after Monday all persons marrying must take the oath before procuring licenses, there was considerable confusion created among certain Confederate Officers, who were looking forward to marriage in the Spring; Such walking as was done on Saturday to get licenses then, and fixing up of old white dresses. . . . There were said to have been 200 marriages in town that day. . . . Tell Carroll B. that we received his letter, and are greatly obligated for his kind invitation, but my coffers are dry; I have not one cent, and no prospect of any unless I go to work. You all don't understand how poor we are here, not even a friend to borrow from, for all are alike.

Mrs. A. Fountain

P.S. Don't let a Yankee see this.

P.S. Mr. Fountain is still in prison; please write to him. I hope he will stop to see you as he comes home, but you must not keep him longer than just to look at him, because I have not seen him for a year. [45]

Agnes _____ Letter to Emilie Anderson, dated May, 1865

Richmond, May, 1865

My dearest Emilie;

. . . I am aggrieved and indignant at the sermons people are preaching to us. . . . War is declared to be a blessing. The high passion of patriotism prevents the access of baser passions. Men's hearts beat together, and woman is roused from the frivolousness and feebleness into her nature is apt to sink. Death, insult, carnage, violated homes, and broken hearts are all awful. But it is worse than a thousand deaths when a people has adopted the creed that the wealth of a nation consists, not in generous hearts, in primitive simplicity, in pretence of duty to life; not in MEN, but in silk, cotton, and something they call capital. If the price to be paid for peace is that wealth accumulates and men decay, far better that every street in every town of our once noble country should run blood.

I feel impatient at this attempt to extort good for ourselves out of the overwhelming disaster which is brought such ruin to others; to congratulate ourselves for what is purchased with their blood. Surely, if for no other reason, for the sake of the blood that has been spilt, we should hasten to acquiesce in the present state of things. . . .

But, now that I have safely boiled over, I will tell you my news. We cannot remain here. We are literally stripped to the "primitive state" state my reverend brother thinks so good for us. We are woefully in need of "silk, cotton, and something they call capital," and we'll never get it here. And so my Colonel and I are going to New York. He has secured a place in some publishing house or other. I only wish it were a dry-goods store.

Of course our social life is over. I have taken my resolution. There are fine ladies in New York A card for a card. A visit for a visit. But I shall imagine not to be recognized. I shall not repine. All the setting, the entourage, of a lady is taken from me, but the lady herself has herself pretty well in hand, and is quite content if she may always be.

Your devoted,

Agnes [46]

Myrta Lockett Avary's Recollections Continue

The confessions of Matoaca:

"I will never forget how queer we thought the dress of the Northern ladies. A great many came to Richmond and Military Headquarters was very gay. Band answered band in the neighborhood of Clay and Twelfth Streets, and the sound of music and dancing feet reached us through our closed shutters.

Some ladies wore on the streets white petticoats braided with black, under their dresses, which were looped over these. Their gowns were short walking length, and their feet could be seen quite plainly. That style would be becoming to us, we said to ourselves—at least I said so myself. Up to that time we had considered it immodest to show our feet, our long dresses and hoop-skirts concealing them. We had been wearing coal-scuttle bonnets of plaited straw, trimmed with corn-shuck rosette. I made fifteen one spring, acquired a fine name as a milliner, and was paid for my work. . . . How eager we were to see the fashions! We had had no fashions for a long time.

When the Northern ladies appeared on the streets, they did not seem to have on any bonnets at all. They wore tiny, three-cornered affairs tied on with narrow string, and all their hair showing in the back. We thought them the most absurd and trifling things! But we made haste to get some. How did we see the fashions when we kept our blinds closed? Why, we could peep through the shutters, of course. Remember we had seen no fashions for a long time. Then, too, after the earlier days, we did not keep our windows shut.

The Yankees introduced some new fashions in other things besides clothes that I remember vividly, one being canned fruit. I had never seen any canned fruit before the Yankees came Perhaps we had had canned fruit, but I do not remember it. Pleasant innovations in food were like to leave lasting impressions on one who had been living on next to nothing for an indefinite period.

I am prospering with my needlework. I sew early and late. My friends who are better off give me work, paying me as generously as they can. . . . Many ladies, widows, and orphans, are seeking employment as teachers. The great trouble is that so few people are able to engage them or pay for help of any kinds. Still, we all manage to help each other somehow.

Nannie, our young bride, is raising lettuce, radish, and nasturtiums, in her back yard for sale. She is painting her house herself (with her husband's help). She is going to give the lettuce towards paying the church debt. She has not else to give. I think I will raise something to buy window-panes. Window-panes patched with paper are all the fashion in this town." [47]

The brass buttons on the old uniforms (all the clothes the men have) "my lord" has ordered to be cut off; but we covered them with crepe instead.

Some of the officers in the village look like gentlemen; and it is almost pitiful, or would be if they were not Yankees to see how they long to have us speak to them. In and around the village there are several beautiful girls, many of them refugees, who have no homes and one is not surprised that these men would like above all things to know them.

The northern women were their dresses so high in the neck, and we wear ours so very low, so low indeed, that we almost show our collar bones, and then wear a tiny little linen collar, at least it is supposed to be linen, but most of our things are not as they seem. But then we had our fashions so long, we don't care to follow theirs. But then we have nothing to follow them with! And have to maintain our confederate motto, "use what we have, and do without what we have not, or invent something to take its place."

The "Button Order" prohibited our men from wearing Confederate buttons. Many possessed no others and had not money wherewith to buy.

Buttons were scarce as hen's teeth. The Confederacy had been reduced to all sorts of makeshift buttons. Thorns from thorn bushes had furnished country folks with such fastenings as pins usually supply, and served convenience on milady's toilette-table when she went to do up her hair. One clause in that monstrous order delighted feminine hearts! It provided as thoughtful concession to all too glaring poverty that: When plain buttons cannot be procured, those formerly used can be covered with cloth. Richmond ladies looked up all the bits of crape and bombazine they had, and next morning their men appeared on the street with buttons in mourning

Somehow, nobody thought about Sam's button; he was a boy, only fifteen. He happened to go out near Camp Grant in his old grey jacket, the only coat he had; one of his brothers had given it to him months before. It was held together over his breast by a single button, his only button. A Yankee sergeant cut it off with his sword. The jacket fell apart, exposing bepatched and thread-bare underwear. His mother and sisters could not help crying when the boy came in, held his jacket together with his hand, his face suffused, his eyes full of rage and mortification.

The provision about covering buttons has always struck me as the unkindest cut of all. How was a man who had no feminine relatives to obey the law? Granted as a soldier, he had acquired the art of being his own seamstress; how, when, he was in the woods or over the roads, could he get scraps of cloth and cover buttons?

But of all the commands ever issued the "Marriage Order" was the most extraordinary! That order said people should not get married unless they took the Oath of Allegiance. If they did, they would be arrested.

There was no appreciable reluctance on the part of the people to take the Oath of Allegiance. They could honestly swear for the future to sustain the Government of the United States, but few, or no decent people, even Unionists, living among Confederates, could vow they had given no "aid or comfort" to one The test-oath cultivated hypocrisy in natives and invited carpetbaggers. A native who would take it was eligible to office, while an honest man who would not lie, was denied a right to vote. . . . A few people had serious scruples of conscience against taking the oath. [48]

CHAPTER NINE
Ladies of the Lost Cause

"Gentle and refined women reduced to abject poverty and no hope of relief."—Mrs. Varina Lee

Isabel (Bel) Maury to Mary (Molly) Maury, Richmond, Virginia

Richmond, January 1, [1866]

My dearest Molly

. . . Saturday before Christmas we were all busy preparing a tree for the children. It was beautiful. On the top were two flags, our Confederate and our battle flag. Gen. Lee, bless his soul, was hung immediately below. . . . Of course, we had eggnog Christmas night, but no company. . . . Today, being New Year's Day, we had numerous calls, though very unexpected to us, as Southern people do not generally receive. Ma said that they did once, when she was a young lady, but since it hasn't been customary. My only objection is that the Yankees not only do it, but abuse the custom, and I want to do entirely different from them. We are a distinct and separate nation, and I wish our customs to be as distinct as we are.

Pa is very gloomy—so many without money, without employment, and no prospect for business. Then the Yankees are taxing us, what our people can't pay, to pay their war debts. Yes, we are drained to pay for being reduced to this slavery. Oh! Molly I feel sometimes I would like to get from under their rule. Do you know a nice fellow who wants a nice wife; then tell him if he will deliver her from Yankee rule, here she is.

But Molly, I would rather abide my fate with one of our noble Confederate soldiers, wait on him, help him battle with poverty and the degradation he has been reduced to by an overwhelming number. But Molly, I must begin the New Year by trying to submit more humbly to His will who loveth whom He chasteneth. I know it is all for our good, though, Molly, I must confess I am blind. I pray faith may open my eyes and better reconcile me to our lot. Molly, it is not myself as an individual I deplore, I could not be so ungrateful for we have a home and other comforts still left us, but the numbers of penniless men and women without any prospects for work, the widows and orphans. Oh, Molly, it makes my heart ache.

The poor servants too, how they must suffer. Mammy came back the other day, with tears in her eyes and begged help, "for God's sake." Molly, you know how comfortable she was here. We got her a good home and I am sure we will never let her want bread when we have it. She told us of hundreds in her condition-and they cannot get work and Southern people haven't the means to help them. Tell me of Yankee philanthropy! The do not care what comes of them, and they say so! . . .

Bel [49]

Mary Tucker Magill's Chronicles Continue

The society of Richmond had never perhaps in its best days boasted the same elements of refinement and cultivation which at present crowded its limits. The whole South had poured its contributions into its lap. Nor was money the "open sesame" to its sacred precincts; ruin was too universal. It comprised all of the beauty, intelligence, and aristocracy of the country. No class or sex had escaped the bosom of destruction. Noble, high-born women who had never before served themselves in the commonest affairs of life, now cheerfully bowed their fair heads beneath the yoke of servitude, and with grateful acquiescence with the degrees of fate, shrank not from the humblest duties whereby the merest necessities of life might be won, and each felt that the sacrifices made were in the cause they loved; They emulated their noble mothers of the Revolution, and surpassed them in their self-denials and sufferings. [50]

Several months have elapsed since the close of the war, and Richmond is but beginning to breathe again after the long paralysis which succeeded its final scenes. It is true that sickly odors are still ascending from the ruins, and where the foundations of houses were dug deepest a sullen cloud of smoke still rises from smoldering fires, continues with strange pertinacity to live on without food to sustain them. But notwithstanding, Richmond's wounded are being patched up, and people begin to talk hopefully of her recovery. Her streets are cleared of their piles of rubbish, and here and there workmen, who have doffed the grey for the mason's leather apron, are repairing the waste places and rebuilding the ruined walls; and to supply the lack of buildings for business, booths are opened and merchandise carried on under canvas within the ruins themselves. The disbanded soldiers have returned to their homes and to walks of private life, and sadly but determined are putting their shoulders to the wheel of fortune, which turns but slowly upon the rugged road they have to travel. The highways are open and travel resumed under restrictions. The exiles are beginning to return, and surely but slowly is the pulse of the nation beginning to throb, and its great heart to beat regularly and naturally, through its wounded are still festering and the blood flowing from every pore. [51]

Myrta Lockett Avary's Recollections Continue

Women who had been social queens, who had had everything heart could wish, and a retinue of servants happy to obey their behests and needing nothing, now found themselves reduced to harder cases than their negroes had every known, and gratefully and gracefully availed themselves of the lowliest tasks by which they might earn enough to buy a dress for the baby, a pair of shoes for little bare feet, coffee or tea or other luxury for an invalid dear one or a bit of any sort of food to replenish a near empty larder.

Life in Richmond was unpleasant. . . . In the winter the unpaved streets were a quagmire. In the summer their dust was pervasive. At night, Richmonders groped their way home from work, often tumbling into deep holes in the streets or falling over the stumps of signposts and telegraph poles that had burned during the fire. The smell of garbage rotting in the street and vacant lots that served as unofficial city dumps made many a neighborhood's air almost unbearable. The stench of privies as well as flush toilets that had not yet been connected with the city sewer system was disgusting in the summer.

The Union army band gave nightly concerts in the Capital Square to encourage the women to leave their houses and attend. "There was not intentional slight or rudeness on our part. . . . We tried not to give offense; we were heart-broken; we stayed to ourselves; and we were not hypocrites; that was all."

When the new governor of Virginia, Governor Pierpoint, viewed Richmond, "the windows of the Spotswood and Monumental were crowded with Northern ladies waving handkerchiefs. Our rightful governor was a fugitive; Governor Pierpont was an alien. We were submissive, but we could not rejoice."

Northerners held socials in each others' houses and in halls; there were receptions, unattended by Southerners, at the Governor's Mansion and Military Headquarters. It might have been more politic had we gone out of our way to be socially agreeable, but it would not have been sincere. Federal officers and their wives attended our churches. [52]

Yankees told my father's Negroes they were free, but they did not accept the statement until "Ole Marster" made it.

I remember the night they were called together in the back yard—a green space with blossomy altheas and fruit—trees and tall oaks around, and the scent of honeysuckled and Sweet Betseys making the air fragrant. He stood on the porch beside a table with a candle on it. I, at his knee, looked upon at him and out on the sea of uplifted faces. Some carried pine torches. He read from a paper, I do not know what, perhaps the emancipation proclamation. They listened silently. Then he spoke, his voice trembling: "You do not belong to me anymore. You are free. You have been like my own children. I have never felt that you were slaves. I have felt that you were charges put into my hands by God and that I had to render account to Him of how I raised you, how I treated you. I want you all to do well. You will have to work, if not for me, for someone else. Heretofore, you have worked for me and I have supported you, fed you, clothed you, given you comfortable homes, paid your doctors' bills, bought your medicines, taken care of your babies before they could take care of themselves; when you were sick, your mistress and I have nursed you; we have laid your dead away. I don't think anybody else could have the same feeling for you that she and I have. I have been trying to think out a plan for paying wages or a part of the crop that would suit us all; but I haven't finished thinking it out. I want to know what you think. Now, you can stay just as you have been staying and work just as you have been working, and we will plan together what is best. Or, you can go. My crops must be worked, and I want to know what arrangements to make. Ben! Dick! Moses! Abram! Line up, everybody out there. As you pass this porch, tell me if you mean to stay; you needn't promise for longer than this year, you know. If you want to go somewhere else, say so and no hard thoughts."

The long line passed. One and all they said; "I gwi stay wid you, Marster."

Presently my father was making out contracts and explaining them over and over; he would sign his name, the Negro would make his mark, the witness sign; and the bond for a year's work and wages or part of the crop was complete. [53]

The daily life of the women of Richmond was driven by surviving in a difficult economy. The war resulted in many widows and in long separated spouses long trying to rebuild their lives. "Although women seemed less inclined after the war to write in their letters or diaries about the intimate details of family life, or how the war had changed marriage and their relations with their children, they did comment at some length about economic, social and racial problems that so often plagued them. Indeed the struggle for survival, a struggle that must have seemed endless in the postwar South, provided the social context for both women and men to redefine—or, more accurately, re-establish "proper" female roles."

In order to provide some income to the families, genteel ladies tutored students and taught classes on the arts and etiquette. Others took in sewing. Some became authors and shared their diaries with the world. [54]

"Our women never were whipped!" I have heard grizzled Confederates say that proudly. "There is a difference," remarked one hoary-headed hero, who, after wearing stars on his collar in Confederate service representing his State in the Federal Congress, "between the political and feminine war-spirit. The former is too often for personal gain. Woman's is the aftermath of anguish. It has taken a long time to reconstruct Southern women. Some are not reconstructed yet. Suffering was stamped too deep for effacement. The Northern women suffered with her Southern sister the agony of anxiety and bereavement. But the Southern had other woes, of which the Northern could have no conception. The armies were upon us. There was devastation. The Southern woman and her loved ones lacked food and raiment, the enemy appropriating what we had and blocked ways by which fresh supplies might come; her home was burned over her head. Sometimes she suffered worse things than starvation, worse things than the destruction of her home. [55]

I quote a letter written by Mrs. Lee to Miss Mason, dated Derwent, Virginia, December, 1865:

". . . My heart sinks when I hear of the destitution and misery which abound further South—gentle and refined women reduced to abject poverty, and no hope of relief."

"Do you know how to make lightbread?" one of our friends inquired, and proceeded to brag of her new accomplishments, adding: "I had never gotten a meal in my life until the morning after the Yankees passed, when I woke up to find not a single servant on the place. There was a lone cow left. I essayed to milk her, but retired in dire confusion. I couldn't make the milk go in the pail to save my life! It squirted in my face and eyes and all over my hair. The cow switched her tail around and cut my countenance, make demonstrations with her hind feet, and I retired. . . ."

. . . another friend wrote . . ." We don't hate the Yankees for thrashing us," they said 'But God knows we hated them for turning our women into hewers of wood and drawers of water". [56]

Facing Further Uncertainty

The future would usher in a new life—for better or for worse. And it looked like for worse as the bewildered Southerners contemplated what appeared to be an ominous future. What was to be their fate? Would their land be confiscated? Would high-ranking officers be hanged or imprisoned? Would the South be the victim of a vengeful North? Should they seek what might promise to be a better life in Brazil or Mexico or Europe? Would they be denied the right to vote or representation in Congress? Would they always be treated with contempt, as second class citizens? What would life be like without slaves? How could they ever recover economically? Would they be humiliated and cowed by a vindictive Northern government? How were their children to be educated? How were they to secure laborers without money to pay wages? How would the newly emancipated blacks behave? Will they be willing to work on shares or become indolent, believing freedom meant never having to work at all? Would their former slaves' newly acquired freedom give rise to insurrections, rapes or murders? And yet, for many Southerners, the most immediate question was where their next meal would be coming from. . . . [57]

As slavery had disintegrated during the war, white women glimpsed the future of Southern race relations. Disliking what they saw and trying to ignore the consequences of Confederate defeat, many fully expected emancipation to be gradual. Surely slavery would be replaced with some other form of forced labor; whites and blacks living and working together in a free society seemed beyond imagination. But regardless of desperate attempts to believe that somehow old way survive, emancipation came. Former slaveholders could hardly consider themselves masters and mistresses any longer and instead had to grapple with the reality of what had once been unthinkable. [58]

Now the freedmen are wandering from place to place, with no abiding home. But however much they might worry about the fate of their former slaves, many white women felt their own emotional trauma more deeply. Mistresses shook their heads in wonder, and in sorrow, over how quickly their slaves had left, how little they had really cared for their owners, how little they accepted the paternalistic ethos. [59]

(ed: The women of the South immediately focused their efforts on honoring the Confederate dead. They formed an organization in the city of Richmond to memorialize them since "There is no country upon whose roll of honor shall be inscribed the names of the Confederate dead." . . . "Dying, they left us the guardianship of their graves." [60]

Myrta Lockett Avary's Recollections Continue

Peculiar interest attached to the inauguration of Memorial Day in Richmond in 1866, when Northerners watching Southerners cover the graves of their dead with flowers went afterward and did likewise. In Hollywood and Oakwood cemeteries, there were some 36,000 Southern soldiers representing every Confederate State. On April 19th, Oakwood Memorial Association was founded and on May 10 the procession of five hundred people walking two and two their arms laded with flowers walked out to Oakwood and strewed those flowers on the confederate graves. On May 3rd, the Hollywood Memorial Association was formed and May 31st was its first Memorial Day The day before, a procession wended its way to the cemetery. The young men of Richmond marched to Hollywood, armed with picks and spades and numbering in their long lines of regulars, remnants of famous companies to the strains of martial music. It was symbolic. The South sought to honor her past in peaceful ways. At the cemetery, the pick and spade bearers divided into squad and companies, and worked all day, raking of rubbish, rounding up graves, planting headboards Old men and little boys helped. Negros faithful to the memory of dead friends and owners were there. Several men in Federal uniforms lent brotherly hands. [61]

Epilogue

Myrta Lockett Avary's Recollections Continue

Richmond, built upon its many hills; the capital of Virginia, the centre of refinement, elegance and hospitality of the olden days, and holding fast it laurels to the latest time; Richmond chosen by a new-born nation of the capital of its new-born country; the spot around which cluster the brightest and darkest hours of the Southern Confederacy, the graves of the dead heroes and the graves of dead hopes—who can ever look upon the footprints of her past without a thrill, or read the pages of her story without a tear. [62]

(ed: The long war was over and their defeat was devestating to the Southerners. They had lost 258,000 men from battle wounds or disease. In addition, 129,000 men were returning home with significant physical or mental disabilities. They had sacrificed everything for their cause.

During the war, the Richmond ladies tried to cling to the trappings of their old social strata. Initially, they embraced the war and the demands for self-sacrifice. However, as the war seemed endless and the years wore on, elevating the needs of the nation over one's own lost its appeal. Indeed, even at the expiration of the men's first terms of enlistments in 1862 and 1863, many wives began to encourage their husband not to re-enlist since they had given enough to the cause. By late 1864, many women were actually encouraging their husbands to desert with increasing effectiveness. The emotional and material deprivation took its toll on the ladies. The grinding hardships that they faced and the continuing challenge to survive produced a new spirit of self-preservation. The rise and fall of battle victories and defeats, the worry about the safety of loved ones, the toll of the war on the South and their own survival placed a choking burden on them. Gone were the days of female subordination and men's responsibility for their women's safety and support.

Devout women still tried to fathom God's purpose during the war and its aftermath. Clinging to religion provided great comfort. With so many families separated, women had taken more and more responsibility for sustaining Southern spiritual life. The churches remained important social centers, especially for women who wanted to swap news with relatives in the army or meet soldiers on leave.

The ladies faced a post war world that had dramatically changed. They lived in the environment of military occupation. However, through their experiences, the ladies had gained a new self-image. This new "identity" assisted them in the challenges they faced in their new world order.

In many cases, their men returned home suffering from sickness and wounds not yet healed in addition to psychological changes due to the war. In other words, the rehabilitation of their husband and brothers became another responsibility of the ladies. The ladies had to deal with the delicate task of rebuilding the psyches of the injured and broken men that had returned from war.

It was now a world without slaves. The loss of their slaves represented a loss of property, wealth and possibly position for the elite women. The more direct result was the need for the assumption of the daily work of domestic life by the ladies. Elite women, who were schooled in the arts and literature, had no idea how to raise children or even cook a meal.

As they struggled to survive in the present, the ladies also viewed themselves as the keepers of the sacred past. They may have had hope for the return of the glory of the South. Many women avoided contact with the Yankees. They refused social invitations and only appeared on the streets in cases of absolute necessity. When they left their houses, they veiled their faces and dressed in black. Few were interested in the progress or politics of Reconstruction. They focused on the development of memorial associations to celebrate their veterans' honor and courage. They wanted to end the veterans' pain of loss or failure and focus on their noble sacrifice and ultimate moral victory. They marked graves and assisted in the return of bodies from the battlefield for proper burial "at home". They established the annual day of mourning, Memorial Day, and built great monuments to their heroes.

While their diaries and memories give us a window into their lives, they can't tell the full story of the ladies. Coming from a male dominated society and dependent upon slaves for their domestic life, they had to adapt to a changing world in the face of tremendous stress. They had constant worries about being attacked by or having their property destroyed by the "invaders" In addition, they worried about the safety of their husbands, sons and brothers, and about the war, the war injured and dead, all in a rumor riddled environment. In the midst of all these worries, the genteel ladies were forced to survive in times of shortages and inflation in an environment that required them to learn the daily tasks of domestic life. The courage and character of these ladies of Richmond should inspire generations to come.

Endnotes

1   Robert W. Waitt, Jr., ed. *Hon. C. Hobson Goddin, Vice-Chairman's Speech.*-Official Publication of the Richmond Civil War Centennial Committee.

2   Constance Cary *Harrison, Recollections Gay and Grave*, p. 56.

3   Ibid., pp. 61-63.

4   Ibid., pp. 82-85.

5   Ibid., pp. 55-56.

6   Ibid., pp. 93-94.

7   Ibid., pp. 96-97.

8   Ibid., pp. 181-188.

9   Rev. J. William Jones, Ed, *Social Life in Richmond*, Southern Historical Papers, Vol. 19, December, 1891 by Edward M. Alfriend, pp. 381-383.

10 George C. Rable, *Civil Wars: Women and the Crisis of Southern Nationalism*, p. 197.

11 Ibid., pp. 196-197.

12 Ibid., p. 198.

13 Harrison, Ibid., pp.201.

14 Ibid., p. 203-204.

15 Phoebe Yates Pember, *A Southern Woman's Story*, p. 15

16 Ibid., pp. 91-92.

17 Ibid., p. 93.

18 Sallie Brock Putnam, *A Richmond Lady: Four years of Personal Observation.* pp. 363-365.

19 Fannie Dickenson, *Fannie E. (Taylor) Dickenson's Diary 1865 April 4*-8 pp 1-3.

20 Mary A Fountaine, *Letter to Marie Burrows Sayre (Cousin) dated April 30, 1865*, p. 2.

21 Ibid., p. 3.

22 Harrison, Ibid., pp.210-211.

23   Pember, Ibid., p. 95.
24   Putnam, Ibid., p. 366-371.
25   Mary Tucker Magill, *Women or Chronicles of the War*, p. 377.
26   Ibid., p. 383.
27   Harrison, Ibid., pp. 211-212.
28   Ibid., p. 215.
29   Dickinson, Ibid., p.4.
30   Pember, Ibid., pp. 91-92.
31   Putnam, Ibid., pp. 372-373.
32   Ibid., pp. 385.
34   Dickinson, Ibid., pp.5-8.
35   Magill, Ibid., pp. 381-382.
36   Ibid., p. 385.
37   Dickinson, Ibid., pp. 8-9.
38   Avary, Ibid., p. 17.
39   Ibid., p. 17.
40   Ibid., pp. 19-22.
41   Magill, Ibid., p. 381.
42   Mrs. M.E. Garthright, *Writings to her Grandchildren*, pp. 1-3.
43   Avary, Ibid., p. 161.
44   Emmie Sublett, *Letter to Emily Anderson, dated, April, 29, 1865, Richmond, Virginia.*
45   Mary A. Fountaine, *Letter to Marie Burrows Sayre, Richmond, Virginia.*
46   Agnes ____, *Letter to Emily Anderson.*
47   Avary, Ibid., pp. 147-149.
48   Ibid, pp. 123-124.
49   Isabel Maury, *Letter to Mary Maury, dated January 1, 1866, Richmond, Virginia.*
50   Magill, Ibid., p. 328.
51   Ibid., pp. 385-386.
52   Avary, Ibid., pp. 107-109.
53   Ibid., pp. 183-185.
54   Rable, Ibid., p. 252.
55   Avary, Ibid., pp. *115-116.*
56   Ibid., p. 189.
57   Marilyn Mayer Culpepper, *Women of the Civil War South*, p. 230.
58   Rable, Ibid., p. 252.
59   Ibid., p. 260.
60   Lizzie Car Daniel, *Confederate Scrap Book*, pp. 124-125.
61   Avary, Ibid., p. 405.
62   Magill, Ibid., pp. 292.

BIBLIOGRAPHY

Alfriend, Edward M., *Social Life in Richmond during the War*, Southern Historical Society Papers 19 (1891), 380-386

_____Agnes, *Letter to Emily. Museum of the Confederacy, Richmond, Virginia*. May, 1865

Avary, Myrta Lockett. *Dixie after the War*. New York: Doubleday, Page & Co., 1905

Avary, Myrta Lockett, *A Virginia Girl in the Civil War 1861-1865*, New York: D. Appleton and Company, 1903

Campbell, Edward D. C. Jr. and Kym S. Rice, Ed. *A Women's War: Southern Women, Richmond, Va.*: The Museum of the Confederacy and the University Press of Virginia, 1997

Chesson, Michael B. *Richmond after the War 1865-1890*, Richmond, Virginia State Library, 1981

Culpepper, Marilyn Mayer. *Women of the Civil War South; personal accounts from diaries, letters and postwar reminiscences*. Jefferson, N.C.; McFarland & Co., 2004

Daniel, Lizzie Cary. *Confederate Scrap-Book*. Richmond, Va. J.L. Hill Printing Co., 1893

Davis, William C. and James F. Robertson, Jr. *Virginia at War*. The University Press of Kentucky, 2009

Dickenson, Fannie E. (Taylor). *Diary*. Virginia Historical Society, Richmond, Virginia. April 4, 1865

Evans, Augusta Jan. *Macaria or, Alters of Sacrifice*. Library of Southern Civilization): Louisiana State University Press, 1992

Faust, Drew Gilpin. *Mothers of Inventions: Women of the slaveholding South in the American Civil War*. Chapel Hill: The University of North Carolina Press, 1996

Faust, Drew Gilpin. *Southern Stories Slaveholders in Peace and War*, Columbia, University of Missouri Press, 1992

Fontaine, Mary. *Letters*. Eleanor S. Brockenbrough Library, The Museum of the Confederacy, Richmond, Virginia. April 30, 1865

Garthright, Mrs. *Writings to her Grandchildren*. Eleanor S. Brockenbrough Library, The Museum of the Confederacy, Richmond, Virginia.

Giesberg, Judith. *Army at Home*. Chapel Hill: The University of North Carolina Press, 2009\

Harrison, Constance Cary. *Recollections Gay and Grave*. New York: Charles Scribner's Sons, 1911

Jones, Katherine M., Editor. Ladies of Richmond, Confederate Capital. Indianapolis; Bobbs-Merrill, 1962

Jones, Rev. J. William. *Social Life in Richmond* by Edward M. Alfriend, Southern Historical Papers. Vol. 19, December, 1891

Kimbal, Gregg D. *American City, Southern Place: A Cultural History of Antebellum Richmond*. Athens: University of Georgia Press, 2000

Lankford, Nelson. *Richmond Burning*. New York, New York: Penguin Books, 2002

Loughborough, Margaret and James H. Johnston. *The Recollections of Margaret Cabell Brown Loughborough*. New York, Hamilton Books, 1911

Magill, Mary Tucker. *Women, Or Chronicles of the Late War*. Baltimore: Turnbull Brothers, 1871

Maguire, Judith W. *A Lady of Virginia. Diary of a Southern Refugee during the War*. Richmond: J.W. Randolph & English, Publishers, 1889

Maury, Isabel. *Letter to Molly*. Eleanor S. Brockenbrough Library, The Museum of the Confederacy, Richmond, Virginia. January 1, 1866

Pember, Phoebe. *A Southern Women's Story: Life in Confederate Richmond*, edited by Bell I Wiley. Jackson Tennessee: McCowat-Press, 1959 [originally published 1879]

Putnam, Sallie A. Brock. *A Richmond Lady. Richmond During the War: Four years of Personal Observation. N*ew York: G.W. Carleton, 1867

Rable, George C. *Civil Wars—Women and the Crisis of Southern Nationalism*. Urbana and Chicago: University of Illinois Press, 1998

Sublett, Emmie. *Letter to Emily Anderson*. Eleanor S. Brockenbrough Library, The Museum of the Confederacy, Richmond, Virginia. April 29, 1865

Thomas, Emory M. *The Confederate State of Richmond: A Biography of the Capital.* Austin: University of Texas Press, 1971

Waitt, Robert, ed. *Centennial Speech.* The Museum of the Confederacy, Richmond, Virginia. May 29. 1961

Weitzel, Godfrey. *Richmond Occupied: Entry of the United States Forces into Richmond, Va., April, 3, 1865* . . . Richmond: Richmond Civil War Centennial Commission, [n.d.]

Woodward, C. Vann, editor, *Mary Chesnut's Civil War.* New Haven: Yale University Press, 1981